ST MARY'S, GREENOCK

The Story of a Community

FRANCES M. DUNLOP

Published by ST MARY'S PUBLISHING in 2001
Cover Design by FRANCES M. DUNLOP and GERARD RALSTON

Printed by GARDNER GIBSON (Print) Ltd., 5 Neil Street, Renfrew PA4 8TA

ISBN 0-954 1556-0-2

St Mary's in 1887.
Painting by Patrick Downie (1854-1945)

Dedicated with love
to the priests and people
of St Mary's,
past, present, and future.

"You are part of a building that has the apostles and prophets for its foundation, and Christ Jesus himself for its main cornerstone. As every structure is aligned on him, all grow into one holy temple in the Lord; and you too, in him, are being built into a house where God lives, in the Spirit." Ephesians 2:20-22

CONTENTS

FOREWORD by Bishop John Mone
ACKNOWLEDGEMENTS
PREFACE

1: Chapels and Car Parks page 9
2: A Whiff of Old Greenock page 15
3: The French Priests page 20
A Greenock Legend
4: The Greenock Mission page 24
5: "Roman Brae" page 32
6: "The Banff Brigade" page 39
7: What Was Life Like? page 45
8: "Priest Danaher" and the "Angel Gabriel" page 51
9: Rev. William Gordon: "Mild, Genial and Gentlemanly" page 59
10: "One of the Finest Churches in Scotland" page 66
11: Changing Times page 71
12: "Education, Education, Education" page 78
13: Rev. Alexander Taylor: "An Ideal Priest" page 84
14: Into a New Century page 92
15: Rev. Patrick Houlihan: "A Sterling Irishman" page 98
A St Mary's Ghost Story
16: War and After page 108
17: The Second World War page 118
18: The Post-War Years page 126
A St Mary's Legend
19: Canon Daniel: "A Man of Much Consequence" page 137
A Code for the Citizen
20: Monsignor Gallagher: "Fifty Years of Loyal Service" page 143
21: Rev. Andrew Carroll: "The Million Pound Man" page 151
22: New Beginnings page 158

APPENDICES — 1: A Chronicle of Events
2: Priests of St Mary's
3: Opening of St Mary's new Church
4: Items gifted to St Mary's Church
5: "The Unremembered"

BIBLIOGRAPHY

FOREWORD

THE BOOK you hold in your hand is the fruit of long hours of research by Frances Mary Dunlop. Those hours have been rewarded in the production of a history of St Mary's Catholic parish in Greenock.

I thoroughly enjoyed reading it. In doing so I learned much, not only about the parish and church of St Mary's, but especially about the parish community.

Inevitably the history is written against the backdrop and within the context of her beloved town of Greenock. It is written with joy and with sadness. It is written with humour, and I had many a chuckle and many a laugh as I read it.

My own French formation meant that I took a special interest in the thread of the French Connection the author develops in relation to Greenock and St Mary's in particular.

I thank Frances Mary for her insightful glimpse of the clergy who served in St Mary's over the past two hundred years. She tells it as it was, and is!

To remember the dedication and enthusiastic faith of those who have gone before us, is so important. Their memory should not be forgotten.

I was grateful to read of the powerful place that education has in the history of the growing Catholic community in St Mary's. The particular recognition of the work of the Franciscan of the Immaculate Conception as educators in Greenock is well merited.

The short chapters filled with fascinating information help to make this history very readable. I hope you enjoy it as much as I have.

+ John Mone.

Paisley, July 2001.

ACKNOWLEDGEMENTS

I SHOULD like to express my thanks to Bishop John Mone, for taking the time to read the draft of this book, and graciously agreeing to write a Foreword. I am particularly grateful to Fr Andrew Carroll and Fr John Tormey for their cooperation and encouragement. Thanks also to Bishop Stephen McGill for his interest in the project; and to Canon Andrew Reid for keeping me right on several points.

Very many people had a hand in bringing this work to fruition, and I should like to record my gratitude to all who have helped in any way. Thanks must go in the first place to Andrew Hanley, whose idea it was to produce a history of St Mary's Parish; and to Mrs Kathleen Stewart, Parish Secretary, for her unfailing patience when I pestered her with questions. Sincere thanks to to all those who contributed information and shared their reminiscences, particularly Canon John McElroy, Canon Denis J. Sheahan, Fr Arthur Kilpatrick R.I.P., Sr Mary Anthony O.S.F., Sr Laurence (Little Sisters), Sr Eleanor S.H.M., Eileen Feen (Legion of Mary), William B. McLellan (S.V.D.P.), Martin McGeehan (Steering Group), Michael McDonald (organ builder), Jean Jeffreys, Alex. Kuszynska, Gerry McLaughlin, Mary McVicar, Peter Mallon, Anne Munn; and to all others who gave or lent treasured documents or photographs: Veronica Brennan, Mary Teresa Burrows, Ella Briceland, Geraldine Doherty, Gertie Gallagher, Margaret Lafferty, Bridget McCann, Rose Macdonald, John McGarry, Kathleen McGarva, Isobel Wilson R.I.P.

For their special help I am grateful to Canon Bernard J. Canning (Paisley Diocesan Archivist); Dr Mary McHugh (Glasgow Archdiocesan Archives); James McKean (Scotus College); Jim Hunter (*Greenock Telegraph*); Lesley Couperwhite (Watt Library); and Diane Mullen, who generously gave me access to her research material on Irish immigration.

I am indebted to Gerard Ralston who helped with photographic work, and with the cover design; and to John Burrows who prepared the manuscript for printing. His expertise was awesome, and his patience boundless. (It had to be!) My thanks also go to Geoffrey Stell and Dr Evelyn Stell for useful suggestions and meticulous proofreading. (I take full responsibility for any mistaks which have crept in subsequently!)

The people of St Mary's, and friends outwith the Parish, have sustained me by their interest and encouragement, which I have greatly appreciated.

Last, but certainly not least, heartfelt thanks to the staff of St Mary's Parish House, to Pauline Davidson for "working lunches", and to Eleanor Brown for countless cups of tea, without which this project could never have been completed!

FMD

PREFACE

THE PROCEEDS from the sale of this book will go to St Mary's Building Fund. After 140 years the "Grand Old Lady of Patrick Street" is showing her age, and requires more than just a touch of make-up to restore her to her former glory.

On 28 June 1907 the *Catholic Herald* quoted Fr Patrick Houlihan's observation that "it was a pleasure to notice on all sides, among rich and poor in the congregation . . . the deep love and regard for the Church of St Mary's (*Applause*) . . . and he had no doubt of the anxious desire and wish of the people of the parish to do what they possibly could to enhance the beauty of their handsome church."

Nearly one hundred years later these words still hold good. Parishioners past and present have been making herculean efforts to raise the required funds, and we look forward to worshipping in our beautifully renovated church.

However, this is the story, not of a building, but of people, the Parish Community of St Mary's, Greenock.

We have come to a special moment in our history. The year 2002 marks the 140th anniversary of the present church building, which was opened in 1862. And in 2008 we will celebrate the bicentenary of the founding of the Greenock Mission from which St Mary's grew.

It has been a fascinating, and at times a deeply moving task to trace our roots back even earlier to the embryo Catholic community of the 1790s.

St Mary's holds a position of immense historical significance, as the Mother Church not only of the former Three Burghs of Greenock, Gourock and Port Glagow, but of a large area of lower Clydeside, stretching from Dunbartonshire to Ayrshire.

I hope reading our story may give enjoyment not only to parishioners of St Mary's, but also to others who are interested in the history of the local area.

There is no such thing as objective history, but only someone's perception of history. This account is a truthful one, but it makes no claim to be unbiased, for it was written with love.

FMD, 15 August, 2001

NOTE

It was not until the late 19th century with its huge influx of Irish Catholics that it became usual to refer to secular priests as "Father" in the Irish fashion.

Previously in Scotland this title was reserved for Regular priests, seculars being addressed as "Mister".

(Secular priests are those belonging to a diocese. Regulars are members of a Religious Order or congregation.)

CHAPTER ONE

Chapels and Car Parks

PAUSE for a moment in the upper part of Greenock's busy, noisy Kilblain Street, watch the coming and going at the bus terminals, the constant stream of cars. It is hard to realise that you stand on hallowed ground.

Here in the heart of St Mary's Parish was the earliest known cradle of Christianity in our area.

Roll back a few centuries, and see in your mind's eye a peaceful spot on a pleasant, wooded hillside, overlooking the river. Although not particularly lofty, this was quite a commanding site, with wide views all around, as just here the hills sweep round to the mouth of the valley of what was later called the West Burn, a sizeable stream in early times. Here stood the chapel, or "cill", of St Blane, its origins lost in antiquity.

Named after the sixth-century St Blane of Bute, perhaps even founded by him, its probable site is now covered by the Hastie Street car park behind St George's North Church. Human remains were found from time to time when building was taking place in the George Square area, probably on the site of the graveyard attached to the chapel. After the Reformation the name Kilblain was perpetuated by a farm, which later still gave its name to the street.

A pleasant and unexpected link to those early days can be found behind the Sheriff Court nearby where you will see the first daffodils making a brave springtime show, a reminder that in medieval times daffodils were planted round churches to ensure a supply of altar flowers for Easter. Can you picture the scene? — the sound of bird-song broken by the ringing of a small hand-bell calling a few fisher and farming folk to the tiny stone chapel, surrounded by "lent lilies".

Established somewhat later, the chapel of St Lawrence[1] stood further east, near the present fire station. It is commemorated in the name of Chapel Street, and it also gave its name to the Bay of St Lawrence, along whose broad sandy shore straggled the row of fishermen's huts from which the town of Greenock eventually grew. The chapel stood at the "Row End", roughly where Safeway's car park now is.

Another small chapel was situated near the present boundary of Port Glasgow. This chapel gave its name to the farms of East and West Chapelton, after which the present-day housing scheme of Chapelton was named. The ancient chapel stood nearer the shore.

There was another at Chrisswell (originally Christ's Well) on the road to Inverkip. This chapel is said to have been founded around 1390, but the old holy well was no doubt revered long before that,

An unlikely sacred spot! The bushes mark the approximate site of St Blane's Chapel.
Photograph by F. M. Dunlop

1. This was the traditional Greenock spelling of the saint's name. It was Canon Daniel in the 1950s who changed to the Latinate spelling of "Laurence". There is a story that the St Lawrence River in Canada was named after our Bay of St Lawrence, but I cannot supply any evidence for this!

even back in pre-Christian times, perhaps. Today its memory is still perpetuated in Chrisswell Farm near the I.B.M.

Before the Reformation Greenock formed part of the large rural parish of Inverkip, stretching from Langbank and Kilmacolm to possibly as far down as Largs. Nothing now remains of the old Parish Church near Inverkip, which was a dependency of Paisley Abbey.[1] This just meant that its revenues belonged to the Abbey.

Chapels in the surrounding district which were not monastic establishments would be served by vicars deputising for the parson at Inverkip.

After the Reformation, from 1560 onwards, Catholicism died out in the area. The chapels may have been demolished, or simply allowed to fall into ruin, although St Lawrence's is said to have been "in high preservation" as late as 1760, being finally demolished some twenty years later.

By 1603 when James Beaton, the last pre-Reformation archbishop of Glasgow, died in France, there seem to have been only about half a dozen priests in the whole of Scotland. From then on the Faith was kept alive by a handful of heroic priests going about the country in disguise, risking imprisonment or banishment, and even death, for the "crime" of saying Mass. They were mainly Franciscans, Vincentians, and Jesuits, and among them was St John Ogilvie, martyred in 1615, who is known to have visited Renfrewshire, which until recently included Inverclyde. Did he celebrate Mass in Newark Castle, which at that time was occupied by the Maxwell family? Or at Castle Levan, then owned by the Semples.

These families were prominent Catholics, repeatedly fined for their stubborn adherence to the Church, and were eventually forced to sell up and leave the district, the Semples in 1649 and the Maxwells in 1694. Without the protection of these powerful families there were few, if any, Catholics left in the whole area which is now Inverclyde, for the pressure to conform was intense. Fines and confiscation of property were inflicted for failure to attend Protestant worship, and without priests the sacramental life withered.

The Scots Colleges abroad were founded to educate a supply of priests for the Home Mission, and in the course of time, and under very difficult circumstances, tiny seminaries were opened, hidden away in the Highlands. Slowly, the dying flame flickered back to life. By 1798 the number of Scottish priests had risen to fifty. Reading of

1. Founded 1169.

the harsh conditions which priests endured in those days, it's a wonder that any of them persevered. We should never forget our debt to them.

Scotland now had the status of a Mission Territory, directly under the supervision of the Roman Congregation for the Propagation of the Faith. The country was divided into two Districts, Lowland and Highland, each under a Vicar Apostolic — the title of a bishop in a missionary country.

* * *

In 1589 the church was built which was later called the Old West Kirk of Greenock. This is said to be the first purpose-built Protestant church in Scotland after the Reformation. Dismantled and moved to the Esplanade in the 1920s to make way for shipyard expansion, it originally stood on the edge of the growing town, at the mouth of the West Burn, with the minister's glebe stretching to the west. (Who remembers the Glebe Sugar House?) You can see the commemorative sign in Container Way opposite the entrance to Tesco's. The approximate site of the church is now occupied by the Mecca Bingo Hall, so you could say it is still a hallowed spot for some! Its car park covers the churchyard which was to be the resting place for a time of Greenock's first priests, this being the original burial ground of the town. (Car parks cover many of Greenock's sacred sites!)[1]

Time passed, the little town grew, a harbour was constructed in 1710, giving a tremendous boost to the town as a trading port. The steady stream of incomers increased dramatically, and the population ballooned in the second half of the 18th century, from 4000 in 1755 to close on 19,000 in only fifty years. They came looking for work from the surrounding countryside of Renfrewshire and Ayrshire.

Many more came from the Highlands, particularly nearby Argyll. In fact by 1793 the most common name in the town was Campbell. Most of the sailors and boatmen were Highlanders, and it was said that you could at times walk from one end of Greenock to the other without hearing a word spoken except Gaelic. After the failure of the Jacobite Rising in 1746 the Highlands suffered from very severe repression, which was to continue throughout the nineteenth century, as landowners began to clear their estates of people to make way for more profitable sheep. Following on bad harvests in the 1770s and

1. In 1927 the priests' remains were removed to Greenock Cemetery.

1780s, the Highlands were devastated by famine, and more and more refugees were heading south, many to sail for Canada on the emigrant ships, but some also to settle in the Lowland towns, including Greenock. There would be some Catholics among those from the far north.

The graveyard of the Old West Kirk — the original burial place of Greenock's earliest priests.
Photograph: Watt Library

A trickle of immigrants from Ireland had already begun, mainly, but not exclusively, Catholic.

In 1786 Bishop George Hay, Vicar Apostolic of the Lowland District, received a letter from his coadjutor,[1] Bishop John Geddes, urging him to establish a Mission in the Glasgow-Paisley-Greenock area, where he estimated that there were now around two hundred Catholics. However, no priest was available till 1792, when the Rev. Alexander MacDonnell, a native of Glengarry, was sent from the Highland District to Glasgow, to care for the Highlanders settled in and around the city. The Glasgow Mission station covered a huge area including Paisley, Greenock, all the way down to Ayr and even further south.

Until then the few Catholics in this area had to depend on occasional visits, mainly from Bishop Geddes himself, who walked all the way from Edinburgh, a kenspeckle figure with his knapsack and the latest in technology - a folding umbrella! Perhaps he bought it specially for trips to Greenock!

After 1792 the Catholics here were served by the Glasgow priests, Mr McDonnell and his successors, Rev. John Farquharson and Rev. Andrew Scott, who later became a bishop and who ended his days in Greenock. With so many other calls on their time they were not able to make very frequent trips to the Lower Reaches, and meanwhile the number of Catholics was growing steadily.

At last, in 1808, it was possible to send a priest, and the Greenock Mission was established. This was the birth of St Mary's Parish.[2]

For some time before this, however, Mass had been celebrated in the town on a more regular basis, since at an unknown date in the 1790s a refugee priest named Capperon arrived from France.

1. A coadjutor bishop is an auxiliary with the right of succession.
2. The Paisley Mission was also established around this time.

CHAPTER TWO

A Whiff of Old Greenock

BY THE end of the eighteenth century Greenock had grown into a thriving little port. The visit of the Tall Ships in the summer of 1999 gave us an echo of what the scene must have been like in the days when the harbour was crammed with sailing ships, and the quaysides were busy with vessels loading and unloading. The Rev Archibald Reid in 1793 could write of "woods of masts" at the Tail of the Bank.[1]

"Let herring swim which trade maintain", so ran the first motto of the town, and it could be said that Greenock grew on the back of the herring! This was the home port of a sizeable fishing fleet, and in foggy weather it would almost be possible for a ship to find its way to harbour by the aroma, for the waterfront area was jam-packed with premises for smoking herring, besides which there were pungent fumes from the tar boilers, not to mention the refuse and ordure piled in the streets and running in the gutters, as was usual in all towns at this period. And it was a noisy place, loud with hammering from iron foundries and the many coopering sheds, where barrels were made for packing cured fish for export.

The original harbour has long ago been filled in, but walk along the Waterfront to the point between the swimming pool and the James Watt College building, where you can look straight up William Street to the Wellpark Mid Kirk, and you are standing on the site of the Mid Quay which divided the old harbour in two.

1. Rev. A. Reid, *Statistical Account of Scotland.*

Greenock's shipbuilding industry had begun, Scott's first yard being already in business at the mouth of the West Burn, on the opposite bank from the Old West Kirk. There were also boat-building yards, and maritime industries such as the manufacture of ropes, sails, chains and anchors. The first sugar houses were already operating. So Greenock's traditional industries were well established.

At this period shipbuilding was not doing very well as so many ships had been captured during the recent war with America! However trade in general had begun to pick up after the wartime depression.

The town had not yet spread much beyond its original extent along the river from the West Burn to the Row End (or Rue End) — from where the neighbouring village of Cartsdyke straggled eastward. Greenock, however, had begun to take on a roughly triangular shape, stretching out along the valley of the West Burn towards the Inverkip Road (which was still a country lane winding up hill and down dale to all the farms along the way). The high road to Gourock, later Union Street and Newark Street, was still a "narrow country road between its hedges of hawthorn and sweet briar roses."[1] The road to Kilmacolm was just a cart track.

Perhaps the abbé Capperon arrived in Greenock by ship, or

Conjuring up the past. The visit of the Tall Ships in 1999 gave a hint of what the old port of Greenock must have been like. ***Photo by F. M. Dunlop***

1. T.W. Hamilton, *How Greenock Grew*, p18.

perhaps he came by stage-coach, in which case his journey would end in Cathcart Square, at the White Hart Inn, which was the terminus for the Glasgow coach.

The Square was the hub of the town. It was at that period still overlooked by the old Mansion House on its crag, where the Well Park now is. Public announcements were made by the Bellman from the steps of the New Kirk (as the Wellpark Mid Kirk was then called). Familiar landmarks of a later period, the Lyle Fountain and the Municipal Buildings did not yet exist. To the east and west ran Cathcart Street and Hamilton Street with their fine buildings and good shops.

The peace was kept by the Town Watchmen who patrolled "in nocturnal perambulation with stick and lantern calling at regular intervals the time of night and the state of the weather".[1] They must have been effective as, according to the *Statistical Account* of 1793, Greenock was "remarkably quiet and regular. Very seldom, even in the night time, is there any disturbance or rioting in the streets."[2]

Peat was still cut in the neighbourhood (Peat Road) and sold in the town. Potatoes grown locally on the sandy soil near the shore cost 6d (*2½p*) a peck. (Hands up those who remember 2 gallons = 1 peck. 2 gallons? 10 litres? — a bucketful.) Potatoes and herring were the mainstay of the poor. Fresh locally caught herring were seven or eight for a (old) penny.

At any one time a proportion of the menfolk would be away at sea, and voyages could last for a year or more. There was panic when it was known that the dreaded press-gang was in town, seeking likely lads for the King's Navy. It sometimes happened that a merchant seaman just off a ship would be brutally abducted before he had even had a chance to go home.

In the closing years of the eighteenth century the town was becoming more and more crowded as the population grew. There was money to be made. For instance "the earnings of the carmen, who ply the quays, are very considerable. The sober among them grow rich; the dissipated drink whisky, neglect their families, and starve their horses."[2] These men were employed carting goods such as sugar or tobacco from the harbour to the warehouses.

Large fortunes were being made by shipowners and sugar-house owners. But the ordinary burgesses of the town were also enjoying prosperity.

1. John Donald, *Old Greenock Characters (Second Series)* p49.
2. Rev. A. Reid, *Statistical Account of Scotland.*

In the country at large more and more of the "middle classes" were receiving some education, and as dissatisfaction began to be felt with the classical education offered by the grammar schools, instruction was sought in practical subjects. "Adventure teachers" opened private schools offering modern languages, commercial arithmetic, and the new experimental sciences.

Already in the 1780s there had been a teacher of French in Greenock. And early in 1798 the abbé Simon Louis Capperon, formerly of Limoges and Paris, applied to the Town Council for premises to use as a schoolroom. He was given the use of an apartment at the Royal Closs in Cathcart Street. Royal Closs (or Close) was a large building owned by the Royal Fishing Company, and leased by the Council to house the town's schools.

M. Capperon was the first resident priest in Greenock since the Reformation, as far as we know. He apparently took lodgings in Market Street, one of the town's main streets at that time, though not one of the most salubrious. It followed approximately the line from Tobago Street along King Street, and on to the rear of the Mid Kirk.

Market Street, where M. Capperon had his French Academy. The area pictured is now occupied by the Central Library and its car park. ***Photograph: Watt Library***

The slaughter-house stood on the site of the telephone exchange in King Street, and there were complaints about the effluent being allowed to flow down the streets "through the greatest breadth of the town" to the river.

In March 1798 the enterprising M. Capperon placed the following advertisement in the *Glasgow Courier* :

FRENCH ACADEMY
MARKET STREET, GREENOCK

M. Capperon begs to inform the public that he proposes to take in boarders from the 1st of next June. Those young gentlemen, who wish to learn French quickly, and who may honour him with their confidence will be constantly in company with three Frenchmen, and by this means make the most rapid progress. The terms of board will be £40 per annum, or in that proportion, and the Boarders at liberty to attend the Grammar and Speaking Classes without any addition to the terms. Those who may be desirous of attending the public Schools of Latin, English, Mathematics, Drawing, etc, will find excellent masters in Greenock at a reasonable rate. The apartments are good and well furnished, and the table will be well supplied. Any of the Gentlemen in Greenock will afford information respecting M. Capperon's character.[1]

It appears from this that the abbé had already been in Greenock for long enough to become well-known and established as a respectable figure.

1. James McGloin, *Some French Refugee Clerics (Innes Review,* Spring 1965*)*

CHAPTER THREE

The French Priests

IT WAS the upheaval of the Revolution that drove the abbé Capperon from France. The "Terror" was unleashed not only against aristocrats, but also against the Church, and many priests and bishops fled to England to escape the anti-clerical fury. It is claimed that at one period there were as many as five thousand French priests in England. In due course some of them made their way north, including our M. Capperon. It would be fascinating to know of his adventures up until 1798, by which time he had finally settled in Greenock.

In 1801 Pope Pius VII signed a Concordat with Napoleon — reluctantly, for clauses had been inserted without his agreement. In particular, the right to appoint bishops was reserved to the State. Some of the refugees returned home after this, but others remained in Britain, refusing to recognise the new regime.

Most of the *émigrés* seem to have led a more or less independent existence, seeing themselves as still under the jurisdiction of their own bishops, and not bothering to apply to the Vicar Apostolic for faculties to say Mass and administer the sacraments. Many never learned to speak much English. However "in their own way they carried on a hidden apostolate by breaking down centuries of prejudice against 'Romanism' and 'Popery' . . . The majority of them supported themselves by teaching, became friendly with the ministers of the Established Church and moved freely in the upper classes of society."[1] Strangely enough, another effect of the French Revolution was the partial easing of the Penal Laws to which Catholics were subject. King and Government were horrified by recent events in France where widespread massacres had taken place and the King and Queen had been beheaded. The Revolutionary Government had declared war on Britain. There were many republican groups in England and Scotland, and the government feared outbreaks of rebellion. The Catholic Relief Act for Scotland was hurriedly passed in 1793 partly to win the goodwill of Catholics, and partly to enable them to serve in the army, which until now Catholics had been barred from doing.

The legal position of Catholics was improved in respect of owning and disposing of property; and it was now no longer a criminal offence to say or hear Mass. In practice, the law had not been strictly applied in recent times, and daily life was not much affected. Catholics were still excluded from public office, and from attendance at the Universities. Only marriages celebrated before a minister of the Established Church were recognised as "regular" under Scots Law. "The fees payable were a serious matter to poor people. Sometimes priests had to find the money for Catholics to be married by ministers."[2]

* * *

"Mr Capron", as he was known locally, taught his classes privately in Royal Closs for some time, before being accepted as a town teacher. By 1803 he was receiving an annual salary of £20 from the Council.

The private pupils in his "Academy" would be from the better-off families in the town. Unlike some of his compatriots he does seem to have made an effort to serve the few local Catholics as a priest. We know that he celebrated Mass and administered the Sacrament of Baptism, and on occasion said Mass in Paisley, where there was as yet no resident priest.

Britain had recently renewed war with France; there was much anti-French feeling in the country, and fears of invasion. One Sunday in August 1803 "Mr Capron" was arrested and taken to Edinburgh Castle on suspicion of being a French spy. Fortunately his

1. Peter F. Anson, *Underground Catholicism in Scotland*, pp 215-216.
2. Ibid p198.

imprisonment lasted only five days, and having satisfied the authorities of his innocence he returned to Greenock.

One of his friends, Matthew Sinnott, an Irishman who had a hatter's business in Greenock, wrote a frantic letter to Bishop Hay, the Vicar Apostolic in Edinburgh, begging him to use his influence to obtain the abbé's release:

> "Sir I maide bauld to throble you and Sir I am sorry that I hav reeson to throble you at this time. You hav harde of our taicher been carrid away from heare on pishon of carring on a carspindance with the inmiie to the determint of this cuntery a thing sir that I am canfident he never thought of anything of the kind as he was quite the revarce in all his acheans . . ."[1]

The letter was addressed, in Matthew's delightfully original spelling, to B. Hay, Black firs wine (Blackfriars Wynd), Edinburgh.

One of "Mr Capron's" pupils was Matthew Sinnott's ten-year-old son Richard, who was to be the first known Greenock-born priest.

Louis Capperon died on 27 September 1805, aged fifty. Let's hope that he found Greenock a comfortable and peaceful haven in his last years after the hardships he must have suffered. Perhaps the kilns of the Greenock Pottery reminded him of far-away Limoges, the renowned porcelain-producing town where he had been curé. It is pleasing to record that his neighbours were kind to him, particularly Mr Kerr, a grocer in Hamilton Street, who sent him gifts of eggs and other provisions. The *Greenock Advertiser* printed a touching tribute: "If integrity and goodness of heart, in union with gentle and amiable manners, constitute the true dignity and excellence of man, Mr Capron will live long in the memory of his numerous friends and acquaintances."

* * *

M. Capperon's work was continued by another French priest who came to live in Greenock some time after 1805. This was the abbé Louis Lemonnier, or Lemoine, as he was known, who had been *vicaire*, or curate, of the diocese of Rouen. He had been teaching in Glasgow from about 1798, one of a number of priests from Normandy living in and around Glasgow at that time.

He had some competition from the Rev. John Dunn, a former

1. James McGloin, *Some French Refugee Clerics (Innes Review,* Spring 1965).

minister in Greenock, who had lost his church because of his "levity of conduct". (He had been seen dancing!) Thereafter he was in charge of the public library, where he taught classes in Latin, French and German. M. Lemonnier indignantly pours scorn on him, as one who can "hardly be supposed to pronounce . . . properly" the French language with its "harmonious sounds, idioms and niceties".[1]

It is known that M. Lemonnier said Mass and heard confessions. He lived for a time in Cathcart Street, moving later to the top of Charles Street (in the vicinity of present-day Charles Place.)

Five years before his death in 1813 he saw the arrival of Mr John Davidson,[2] the first official "Missionary Rector" of Greenock, as opposed to the "free-lance" Frenchmen.

A GREENOCK LEGEND

A precious piece of local folklore that ought not to be forgotten:

It was around this time — the early nineteenth century — that our neighbours in Port Glasgow began to taunt us with the jibe, "Who hung the monkey?"

The story goes that a ship put into dock with a pet monkey on board — a very smart monkey, elegantly dressed by the doting crew. The monkey jumped ship and escaped into the town where he encountered some of the natives.

This was at the height of the Napoleonic scare, and faced with this diminutive dandy, chattering in an unintelligible gibberish, arms waving in expressive gestures, the douce burghers of Greenock panicked, and lynched the "French spy". The unfortunate monkey was strung up in the Square.

This tragic tale is not so well known nowadays as it deserves to be. However, if any Portonian of your acquaintance should sneer, "Who hung the monkey?" remember to reply, "Who bil't the bell?" But that's another story!

1. James McGloin, op. cit.
2. It was not until much later that priests in this country were addressed as "Father". See Prefatory Note.

CHAPTER FOUR

The Greenock Mission

REV. John Davidson arrived in Greenock towards the end of the year 1808, and took up residence in the middle flat of a house in Market Street, near the slaughter-house. Next door to the priest's lodgings was the jail, with 30 cells for offenders, and five for debtors. No doubt Mr Davidson visited those members of his flock who were his next-door neighbours from time to time! The site where John Davidson once lived is, yes, another car park — the one behind the library.

The new Missionary Rector was, it seems, born around the year 1765 in the Enzie[1] District of Banffshire, an area which had remained Catholic after the Reformation, and supplied many priests (close on fifty) for the Scottish Mission throughout the eighteenth century.

John Davidson spent two years (1777-1779) at the "hidden seminary" of Scalan in the Braes of Glenlivet, now a revered place of pilgrimage, a memorial to those difficult times. He continued his studies at the Royal Scots College in Valladolid, and after his ordination in Edinburgh was sent back to his native north-east. After short spells in Buchan and Tombae (Glenlivet), he spent ten years in the rugged district of Auchindoun in Glenfiddich. In these glens they produce more than one kind of holy water!

From 1804 till 1808 he was a professor at the seminary of Aquhorties in Aberdeenshire which replaced Scalan.

By the time Bishop Cameron entrusted him with opening the new

1. Pronounced "Ing-ie".

Mission at Greenock he was in his early forties, a mature and experienced priest.

We can imagine with what enthusiasm the new Mission Rector took up his task, no doubt eager to get organised by Christmas. He rented the Star Hall in Broad Close, where he celebrated Mass.

The vestige of Broad Close is marked today with a commemorative plaque, showing where the town jail stood at an earlier period. The Star Hall is said to have been about halfway down on the left hand side. This would make it approximately where Kwik-Fit now stands.

* * *

In November that year Eliza Collins, a Protestant girl, agreed to a Catholic wedding with her soldier sweetheart, Peter Gavie. The record of their marriage is the very earliest entry in our parish register, in Mr Davidson's rather flamboyant eighteenth century handwriting:

> *"This sixteenth day of November one thousand eight hundred & eight I, the undersigned Cath. Clergyman, having got the certificate of the Sesso Clerk that they had*

Broad Close. In 1808 it was not so dilapidated! The Star Hall was half-way down on the left-hand side.
Photograph: Watt Library

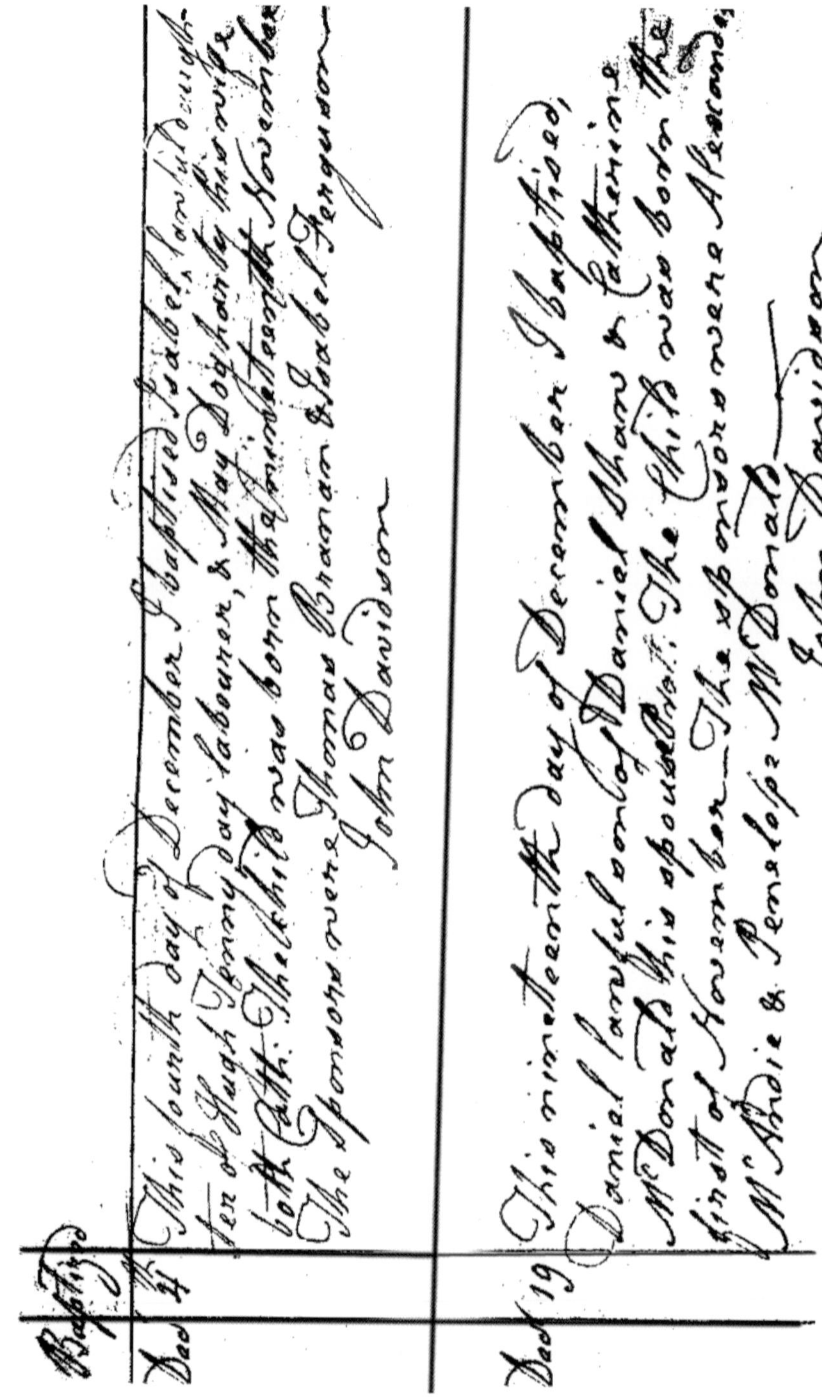

Baptized

Decr 4 This fourth day of December I baptised Isabel, lawful daughter of Hugh Jenny, day labourer, & May Doghorty his wife both Cath: The child was born the nineteenth November. The sponsors were Thomas Brannan & Isabel Ferguson
John Davidson

Decr 19 This nineteenth day of December I baptized Daniel lawful son of Daniel Shaw & Catherine McDonald his spouse Cath: The child was born the first of November. The sponsors were Alexander McArdie & Penelope McDonald
John Davidson

An extract from the first page of the Baptismal Register, started by Rev. John Davidson on 4 December, 1808.

been regularly proclaimed & no objections offered, married, according to the rites of our Holy mother the Church, Peter Gavie Cath: private in the 2nd Battn. of the 71st Regt. & Elizabeth Collins of the New parish Greenock Prot. before these witnesses Bryan Reilly & Joannet McLauchlan — John Davidson."

Soon afterwards came the first baptisms:

"This fourth day of December I baptised Isabel, lawful daughter of Hugh Tenny day labourer, & May Dogharty his wife both Cath. The child was born the nineteenth November. The Sponsors were Thomas Brannan & Isabel Ferguson."

A few days later he baptised Daniel, the baby son of Daniel Shaw and his wife Catherine McDonald. The sponsors were Alexander McAndie and Penelope McDonald.

The names in these early entries demonstrate the make-up of Greenock's Catholic population at that time — mainly Highlanders and Irish.

Unlike his immediate successors, Mr Davidson also recorded the deaths which took place during the six years of his Rectorship, beginning on 12 January 1809 when he noted the death of *"Michael Darroch in Port Glasgow, by a fall down a stair."*

These entries are interesting as he gives the cause of death, and the occupations of the men (but not the women). Most were *"day labourers"* or *"workmen"*; many were sailors. There were many deaths from fever, two cases of consumption, and quite a high proportion of accidental deaths, including two poor men who were run over by loaded carts, and a quarry accident in which two men were killed. There were several drownings, such as the magnificently named Dionysius Swinnie, *"a day labourer (who) fell over the quay in Port Glasgow and was drowned."* Most died *"having received all the sacraments"*. An exception was an unfortunate man *"who was murdered in the street"*.

The numbers of baptisms show the growth of the Mission during these years:

1809 : 44 baptisms
1810 : 70
1814 : 92

* * *

As well as Greenock, the Mission included Port Glasgow, Gourock, and a wide area round about, from Dumbarton down into Ayrshire. Mr Davidson usually had a congregation of about a hundred. The Sunday gatherings in the Star Hall would be very different from the well-dressed, well-fed, sweet-smelling congregation of present-day St Mary's. For although there were a few Catholics among the better-off, like Matthew Sinnott, most were the poorest of the poor. Apart from the priest, not many would have shoes. Some would be suffering from rickets and other ailments due to poor nutrition. Not a few would be lousy. (Indeed, Robert Burns tells us that even the "better classes" could harbour "little visitors" - just read "To a Louse"!) And yet they were just like us, meeting on a Sunday for the same purpose.

The priest shared his people's poverty. From the bishop's common fund he received £10 per annum, which even in those days was not much of a wage, and what he received from his congregation would not amount to very much. (The ministers were better off! In 1793 the minister of the Old West Kirk was receiving an annual government stipend of 100 guineas, exclusive of manse and garden.)

Mr Davidson supplemented his income by giving Spanish lessons in John Dunn's school.

We can imagine what a motley crew our spiritual ancestors were: boatmen, dockers, fishwives, servant lasses (these would consider themselves a cut above the rest), factory workers (including quite young children), street musicians, peddlars, beggars. There would also be a sizeable floating population (literally!) of visiting sailors from foreign parts, fishermen from as far away as the Isle of Barra down to sell their dried cod and ling, possibly some seasonal agricultural workers from Ireland, employed at some of the outlying farms: Bow Farm, Strone Farm, Holmscroft, Drums . . . and all the other varieties of human being that would pass through a busy seaport.

When they arrived in the Star Hall for "Prayers", their experience was very different from what we are used to nowadays. Proceedings would start with a (long!) sermon, followed by (long!) prayers, including Acts of Faith, Hope and Charity. The priest then celebrated Mass, generally as quickly as possible, in the way that had become the norm in the days when a priest could expect to be arrested if he was caught saying Mass.

One wonders how comprehensible all this was. It cannot have been easy for John Davidson and his flock to understand one another, he being a Banffshire loon, and they being a motley assortment speaking broad Clydeside, or else nothing but Scots or Irish Gaelic. Not to mention the many visiting foreign seamen.

At this period, the early nineteenth century, all classes of society in the Lowlands spoke broad Scots of one variety or another, though the intelligentsia, like Robert Burns, could speak and write perfectly good English. In the days before mass communication, the local dialects were much broader, and markedly different from one another. The priests spoke their own version of Scots, like Bishop Andrew Scott at a slightly later date, who despite many years' residence in Glasgow and Greenock, spoke broad Banffshire till his dying day. So very likely the vernacular sermon and prayers would be as incomprehensible to the congregation as the Latin of the Mass. Even today the broadest Banffshire is quite difficult for a Greenockian to follow. (Experience speaks!) Perhaps they got used to it in time.

During Mass some of the people would probably recite the Rosary, or, if they could read, would use a book of Devotions, such as the English Bishop Challoner's *"Meditations During Mass"* which was popular in Scotland at that time.

There was no music or singing, this being considered unsuitable for Catholic worship. The Vicar Apostolic, Bishop George Hay, was very strict in this regard. He appears to have thought it unseemly. Besides, he had been deeply traumatised by the No-Popery riots which swept the whole country back in the 1770s when the first moves had been made to relax the laws against Catholics. Since then his policy had been for Catholics to keep a very low profile. This was why, for instance, Mass was referred to as "Prayers". Now that life was a little bit easier, and Catholics were generally regarded with less suspicion, he was terrified of the trouble that might be stirred up if Catholics started drawing attention to themselves by breaking the Sabbath calm with loud singing!

In a few places efforts were being made to make the Liturgy more attractive by introducing some music. A "short, stout, merry little monk"[1] called Fr Gallus Robertson, who was chaplain to some of the Catholic gentry in Galloway, had the people "singing and ranting psalms of his own translation"[1] What an innovation! He was far ahead of his time! At Christmas 1789 the priest of the Highland Chapel in Edinburgh allowed his congregation to sing "Adeste Fideles". Wow!

1. Peter F. Anson, *Undeground Catholicism in Scotland*, p200-201.

However, these experiments were stopped as soon as the Bishop got wind of them! "I must and do insist . . . on your giving up your singing. If this occasions any trouble to yourself, you have only yourself to blame for it, from the rash step you have taken, and you must extricate yourself the best way you can"[1], he wrote to Fr Gallus. It was not until after Bishop Hay's death in 1811 that a few liturgical changes were sanctioned by his successor, Bishop Cameron.[2]

* * *

M. Lemonnier died in 1813. There is no record of him saying Mass publicly after Mr Davidson's arrival, but he had been a regular attender at Mass in the Star Hall. He was buried in the Old West Kirkyard, in the family lair of that good soul, Matthew Sinnott.

1813 saw the arrival of another Norman priest, M. Gilles-Vincent Despréaux, a former professor of Latin at the Collège d' Avranches. He had latterly been teaching in Paisley, and now opened a French Academy in Greenock. Apparently Greenock was not to his taste, however, and he soon returned to Paisley. He seems to have been rather a difficult character. He quarrelled with Bishop Cameron, who threatened to withdraw his faculties for saying Mass. (Certainly Greenockians must have thought him a bit strange, preferring Paisley to Greenock!)

The Catholic population continued to grow, and in 1814 Mr Davidson began the first St Mary's Building Fund to erect a church and school. In less than two years the sum of £216 7s 2d was contributed, an amazing total, given the poverty of the people. A pleasant site was acquired in East Shaw Street, on the edge of town, and building began.

Sadly, John Davidson did not live to see the completion of his great project. He died on 8 January 1815, and according to the later memoirs of Canon Michael Condon, he "had the biggest funeral ever seen in Greenock". The *Greenock Advertiser* (13 January 1815) calls him "a man of unaffected piety, assiduous in his duty as a clergyman, benevolent and attentive to the poor."

Like his French predecessors, he was buried in the Old West, through the charity of the Sinnott family. (Later, when the kirk was moved, the priests were re-interred in Greenock Cemetery. This took

1. Peter F. Anson, *Undeground Catholicism in Scotland*, p200-201.
2. Although in this matter he was a bit of a killjoy, I would not wish to give an unfavourable impression of Bishop Hay, who was one of the outstanding figures of the Church in the eighteenth century. A convert, he led a fascinating and adventurous life since as a young medical student he helped to tend the wounded after the Battle of Prestonpans. Under his leadership the Catholic Church in Scotland began to "emerge from the Catacombs".

place on 16 March 1927.) It was left to his successor to complete the building of the first St Mary's.

* * *

On 9 January, the day after Mr Davidson's death, there is an entry in the baptismal register: *"Greenock having no proper pastor, was baptised by the undersigned John, infant son of Ronald Griffith and Catherine Dunlevy."* (Unfortunately the baptiser forgot to add a signature.) The baby had been born that same day. In naming their baby, were Ronald Griffith and his wife paying tribute to a well-loved priest?

Fr John Tormey, Parish Priest of St Mary's in 2001, examining the stone which commemorates his predecessors. The inscription records: *The remains of Rev Father Lemoine and Rev Father Davidson were transferred from Old West Kirkyard to Greenock cemetery on 16th March, 1927.*
The last resting place of M. Capperon is unknown. (See Appendix 5). ***Photograph by F. M. Dunlop***

CHAPTER FIVE

"Roman Brae"

UNDER the new Rector of the Mission, Rev. John Gordon, building work proceeded rapidly. 1815 was an eventful year. Napoleon's defeat at Waterloo in June brought peace at last to Europe. And by Christmas the Catholics of Greenock were able to worship in a proper church. Dedicated to Our Lady, it stood at the corner of East Shaw Street and Bearhope Street, which was thereafter nicknamed the "Roman Brae"! There was seating for approximately 400 in the fairly plain interior.

Sunday, 25th August, 1816: a high day in the annals of St Mary's, when Bishop Alexander Cameron came to perform the official opening. Mr Gordon had inserted a notice in the paper, inviting all to attend and to help by their contributions; and indeed the *Greenock Advertiser* reported that "a crowd of strangers assembled to witness the ceremonies of the day, who were accommodated to the utmost extent that the limits of the church would admit. The Right Rev. Bishop, in a highly animated, eloquent, and appropriate address . . . expressed his most grateful acknowledgments for the tolerance in matters of religion now so conspicuous in the country, and in no part more so than in the West of Scotland." The Bishop took as his text the parable of the Good Samaritan, and "sought to instil into the minds of all the mutual obligations which bind man to his fellow-man, developing in the most luminous manner the order of charity which ought to exist in all our social relations."

The *Advertiser* article concludes on the happy note that "the

Old St Mary's, East Shaw Street. This picture first appeared in the 1897 Bazaar Handbook.

Drawing by Fr Alexander Murphy, O.S.F.

An impression of the interior of Old St Mary's, based on St Mary's, Kirkconnell, New Abbey, Kirkcudbright, which was typical of chapels of this period. (1816).

Drawing by Tom Robinson, based on a sketch by Peter F. Anson.

collection obtained at the door of the chapel was, we understand, liberal."

Psychologists will tell you that praising desirable behaviour tends to "effect what it signifies", in other words it makes people more likely to adopt this behaviour. There may have been an element of this in the bishop's tribute to the tolerance which prevailed. Having said that, a striking motif in the story of St Mary's throughout the years is the good relations which existed for the most part with members of other denominations. Not all local communities were so tolerant of the opening of a new Catholic church.

The same year, 1816, saw the opening of St Andrew's, Glasgow, later to become the Cathedral. Rev. Andrew Scott, in charge of the Glasgow Mission, had big ideas! With 3,000 souls in his care, he determined to give them a worthy place of worship. He persevered despite great difficulties, and in the face of many warnings against erecting such a large and flamboyant "Mass House" in a prominent position on the bank of the Clyde. Just asking for trouble. In fact, many a night his opponents tried to pull down what had been built during the day. When at last St Andrew's was completed, it was hailed as "the most magnificent and most spacious Papist place of worship in the whole of Britain."[1]

We shall hear more of the intrepid Mr Scott.

Meanwhile, Mr Gordon continued to raise funds for the building of the school. A famous preacher, Fr Murphy from Dublin, was invited to preach a charity sermon, which raised the handsome sum of £21.16s.8d (*£21.84p*).

St Mary's school was opened on Saturday 11th October, 1818 by Bishop Paterson, who celebrated High Mass in the church.

* * *

The little complex on "Roman Brae" now consisted of church, school, teacher's house and priest's house.

The town centre was now becoming more and more congested as newcomers continued to pour in seeking work. Some of the leading citizens still lived in the centre, but the more prosperous had for some time been moving out to the surrounding countryside where they built large mansions with the fortunes they made from industry and trade (including, it must be said, the slave trade).

1. Peter F. Anson, *Underground Catholicism*, p230.

One of the earliest of these grand houses is the elegant Georgian mansion which is now the Tontine Hotel. When it was built in 1805 it was the most westerly building in the town, surrounded by fields. It stood on the High Road to Gourock, and its extensive grounds sloped down to the river. It had its own water supply too — the house was built over a well. Previously the site had been occupied by a windmill for grinding corn.

The vacated houses in the town centre were sub-divided, the large gardens were built on. These were the notorious "back lands", a higgledy-piggledy shanty town of ramshackle tenements, threaded by a warren of narrow, stinking lanes. Here lived most of the Catholics in Greenock in the early part of the nineteenth century — mainly poor Irish immigrants.

There was no sanitation; water had to be carried from wells, such as the Long Well in what is now Duff Street. If there was no well nearby, you could buy from the water carts which trundled through the streets. Little wonder that although the town was considered to be "not unhealthy", fevers and smallpox "among the lower sort of people . . . are sometimes fatal".[1]

For the upper ranks of society there was ample opportunity to participate in the vigorous cultural life of the Enlightenment. Scotland's oldest subscription Library had been founded in Greenock in 1783. In 1800 the composer Neil Dougal began putting on his annual concerts, at which he and his pupils performed. In the same year the young John Galt, a clerk in a local shipping office, founded the Literary Society. The world's first Burns Club had been founded in 1801. As early as 1806 it was presenting prizes to schoolchildren for performing the works of Burns and other Scottish poets. There was also a theatre in the town.

* * *

John Gordon was a brilliant scholar. As a student he had been sent from the seminary at Scalan to the Scots College in Rome at the age of only ten, since he had made such progress in his studies. He was in Rome at the time of the invasion by Napoleon, when the College was occupied by French troops, and the students had to be evacuated back to Scotland. After ordination he taught at the new seminary of Aquhorties, where Mr Davidson was also on the staff.

1. Rev. A. Reid, *Statistical Account of Scotland.*

Mr Gordon was there for thirteen years before being sent to Greenock, so this was his only mission posting. He was remembered as a powerful preacher. Like his predecessors he also worked as a teacher, advertising classes in French, Italian, Latin, Greek, Geography and Mathematics.

His health was never good. Right from the earliest years of his ministry in Greenock there are entries in the Registers by Rev. Andrew Scott from Glasgow, and other visiting priests, who performed baptisms "during the illness of the proper pastor" . . . "Mr Gordon, the proper pastor being unable from indisposition".

* * *

From time to time in the early years he had the assistance of the Rev. Dr Richard Sinnott, who was the first Greenock-born priest, as far as we know. Richard's father Matthew was a prosperous businessman, who could afford to give his younger son a good education, including French lessons from abbé Capperon. Richard studied medicine at Edinburgh, despite the fact that Catholics were still officially barred from Scottish Universities. It seems that by now the law was not being strictly applied. On completing his medical studies he entered the seminary at Aquhorties and was ordained at Edinburgh in 1817. After two years' pastoral work in Edinburgh and Terregles (near Dumfries) he was back at the seminary, where he taught for the next six years.

During this period entries by him in St Mary's Parish Registers show that he made fairly regular visits home to Greenock to see his family. We can catch intriguing glimpses of his family life from the Registers: we can imagine him visiting his sister Anne, her husband Finlay Shields, and their daughter Mary, born in 1809. His older brother Mathew *(sic)* (Did he inherit the hatter's business?) was married to Mary Taylor. Their first baby Mathew was baptised on 15 February 1818; their second son Richard, twelve days old, was baptised by Mr Gordon on 5 December 1819. The godfather was the child's uncle, Rev. Richard.

After his stint as seminary professor, Richard was to spend the next twenty-five years in Galloway, at Stranraer, and then at Newton Stewart, where he opened a new mission. He was responsible for a huge area of nearly 1000 square miles.

* * *

No doubt Mr Gordon appreciated the assistance of the younger priest. One gets the impression of a man struggling with ill-health for many years. And yet he laboured on in Greenock for 17 years, when perhaps by temperament he was more suited to an academic life.

As well as Greenock, he was, of course, responsible for a wide area from Dumbarton to Ayrshire, in the days when travel was not the simple matter that it is now. During the year 1815, for instance, Mr Gordon travelled far afield to carry out baptisms in Port Glasgow, Dumbarton, Ayr, Saltcoats and Irvine.

By 1830 the Catholic population of Dumbarton had increased to the point where it could become a viable independent Mission. Mr Gordon undertook the building of its church — St Patrick's.

The first resident priest was Rev. John Gifford, who stayed with Mr Gordon in Greenock until his new house in Dumbarton was completed.

By 1832 Mr Gordon's health was breaking down completely, and he was sent an assistant, Rev. Joseph Curr, "an English priest of means and gentle blood".[1] He didn't stay long, as he had a dispute with some of the congregation, and walked out after only a few months. He was replaced by Rev. William Gordon.

Not long afterwards John Gordon resigned from his post. He retired to Edinburgh where he died on 26 October 1833. He was by no means an old man, being aged only about 54. Old priests were a rarity in those days.

Before his death he saw some momentous changes taking place. From now on the Catholic population continued to increase greatly, particularly in Glasgow and Clydeside, due to the large and ever-growing influx of Irish. Because of this, permission was now sought from Rome to divide the Scottish Mission into three Districts, Northern, Eastern and Western. This took place in 1827. Bishop Ranald Macdonald of the former Highland District was appointed Vicar Apostolic of the new Western District, with Rev. Andrew Scott of the Glasgow Mission being appointed as his coadjutor. He was consecrated bishop in St Andrew's, Glasgow on 21 September 1828. To him fell the care of the now mainly Irish Mission in the southern part of the new Vicariate, while Bishop Macdonald residing on the island of Lismore near Oban, took responsibility for the Gaelic speaking West Highlands.

Then in 1829 the "Act for the Relief of His Majesty's Roman

1. Memoirs of Canon Michael Condon, p229.

Catholic Subjects" was passed, granting Catholic Emancipation. Catholics now had almost the same civil rights as their fellow-citizens, but there were still a few restrictions, for instance, Catholics still could not enter an English or Scottish University. Priests were forbidden to wear clerical dress out of doors; and membership of a male religious order was an offence punishable by a fine or imprisonment in Scotland. These and other sanctions were lifted later, except for one discriminatory provision which still remains in the Statute Book: the Sovereign may not be a Catholic, nor be married to a Catholic. There has been some agitation in recent times for this manifest injustice to be amended, but perhaps it is not something that most of us lose a lot of sleep over.

CHAPTER SIX

The "Banff Brigade"

IN MAY 1832 Rev. William Gordon arrived in Greenock, to assist his namesake, the ailing John Gordon, who soon thereafter retired to Edinburgh, leaving the new young priest in sole charge.

William Gordon was born in Tomintoul on 24 January 1808 (the year of Mr Davidson's arrival in Greenock). He belonged to the notable Banffshire family of Gordons of Glenbuchat, prominent in Jacobite history. The *Dictionary of National Biography* calls them "a tribe of reivers and the terror of the district", "monsters of wickedness". The story of William Gordon will show that it doesn't do to generalise!

He studied for the priesthood at the seminary of Aquhorties in Aberdeenshire, where in a nice tie-up of fate he was taught Latin and French by Rev. Richard Sinnott, who learned his French from M. Capperon in Greenock. William was then sent to the Royal Scots College, Valladolid. On completing his studies he returned home without being ordained as he was too young at only twenty-one. He was appointed to teach at the newly opened St Mary's College Blairs, which replaced the seminary at Aquhorties.

He was ordained on 4 February 1831 by Bishop James Kyle, in the Church of St Gregory, Preshome, near the town of Keith. This beautiful and historic building was the first post-Reformation place of Catholic worship in Scotland to be built openly to look like a church. It was the headquarters of the Vicars Apostolic of the Northern District.

A few months later came the posting to Greenock.

The new priest was young, only 24 years old, handsome, enthusiastic, and highly gifted — "a neat, smart, lively specimen of humanity."[1] He also had great personal charm, and soon endeared himself not only to his own flock, but to the wider community. In particular, he struck up a warm friendship with with the Rev. Dr James Melville McCulloch, a well-respected minister of the town.

In the same year as Mr Gordon's arrival in Greenock, Bishop Andrew Scott succeeded as Vicar Apostolic of the Western District on the death of old blind Bishop Macdonald. Shortly afterwards he consecrated as his coadjutor bishop another Banffshire man, Rev. John Murdoch. Thirty years later Bishop Murdoch was to open the new St Mary's Church in Patrick Street.

* * *

In 1834 Bishop Scott moved his residence to St Mary's in Greenock, which was a convenient base for his frequent trips to the Highlands.

Bishop Andrew Scott

The Highland and Lowland (now increasingly Irish) divisions of the Western District were completely different in their make-up and their needs. As his predecessor had done, Bishop Scott now decided to concentrate his attention on the West Highlands, leaving Bishop Murdoch in charge of Glasgow and the Lowlands.

The Highlands were in a desperate state, still reeling from the upheavals of the eighteenth century, and suffering the brutal Clearances of the nineteenth. Most of the existing chapels were in a ruinous state and the priests were living in conditions of dire poverty. In a letter written in February 1835 Bishop Scott describes six of the Highland missions: "In every one . . . the walls have been built with dry stone, thatched with turf and heath. Part of the walls

1. Quoted in Memoirs of Canon Michael Condon p269.

have fallen down and half the roofs are blown away."[1] So tumble-down was the chapel on the island of Eigg, that the priest wrote: "During divine service I am constantly distracted by pigs, hens &c."[1]

Obviously a huge building programme was long overdue. All supplies and building materials had to be brought by sea, mostly from Greenock, which was the main port of supply for the West Highlands. So to Greenock Bishop Scott went, with only half-a-crown in his pocket to pay his passage from Glasgow.

The bishop lived in East Shaw Street until his death twelve years later, though he was frequently absent, travelling in the Highlands, sometimes for months at a time, seeing for himself what conditions were like, encouraging and supporting, supervising building work, negotiating for new sites with unfriendly landowners.

From Greenock he was in constant correspondence with the Highland priests, not only sending them building supplies, but doing their shopping for them. He received frequent requests for the likes of "2 lbs. tea", "42 yds. lilac cotton for curtains", "a bread pan for the dutch oven".[1]

By his fatherly interest he restored morale among the priests and people of the Highlands.

* * *

Meanwhile the number of St Mary's parishioners still continued to grow, and no doubt the Bishop's assistance was very welcome when he was actually in town and not off on his travels. Mr Gordon was a devout and gifted young man, but as yet inexperienced in pastoral work. He benefitted greatly from the counsel of the wise old bishop.

Although the worst years of famine in Ireland were still in the future, and the tide of emigration had not yet reached its peak, such numbers of mainly destitute Irish were flooding into Britain as to pose a serious problem for the authorities. A Royal Commission was set up to investigate "The State of the Irish Poor in Great Britain". Mr Gordon's report to the Commission in 1834 makes fascinating reading:

"I calculate the number of my congregation in Greenock at about 4000, of whom all within *(i.e. except)* about fifty are Irish. I judge only from the number of baptisms, which was 174 in 1833. In this

1. Quoted by Rev. Roderick Macdonald, *Bishop Scott and the West Highlands, Innes Review* (Autumn 1966).

number are included the baptisms of Port Glasgow, the Catholic population of which I ascertained . . . to be 369 souls, all Irish, as far as I am aware. All the Catholics in Greenock who are not Irish are Highlanders. The Irish in this town belong almost exclusively to the working classes; there are a few small shopkeepers, some cloth merchants, some brokers, and some provision sellers. Many of them are also hawkers; but these do not stay constantly in Greenock; the rest are labouring men, many of whom work at the quays, loading and unloading vessels; others are engaged by the farmers in the neighbourhood in their improvements in agriculture; a good many work as ships' carpenters; a great many are engaged in the sugar manufactories; some in the foundries. The Irish are treated in this town with a kind of exclusive policy, principally by the lower classes: I do not think there is that feeling among the higher classes; the lower classes consider them as a distinct class of persons. The religious prejudice may probably also contribute something; this is now fast wearing away. The Orangemen and Catholics retain a kind of enmity towards one another; but I have not observed it lead to any overt acts . . .

"There is a kind of advance to an assimilation of feeling with the Scotch in the children of the Irish born in this country, which I attribute mainly to their education. The children chiefly learn the idiom of the town where they are born . . . We have a school of our own, where we educate the children of our own congregation; the attendance is about 120 a-day. Many of them, on account of the poverty of their parents, are forced to work during the day, and for these there is an evening school . . .

"The Irish in this town certainly have the will to assist one another in times of distress or sickness, as far as their abilities will permit them. They often harbour friends, relations, and neighbours when they first come from Ireland, before they can get work. They sometimes invite their own relations if they be destitute at home; generally the young come first, and, if they succeed, they send for the other members of their families, chiefly their parents, in order to support them. There is a great deal of family affection among them; making allowance for their poverty, they appear to me to pay every attention to their children . . .

"During my residence at Greenock the Irish have shown no disposition to disturbance or riot; nor have they taken a more prominent part in trades' union, or combinations of any kind, than the Scotch."

* * *

Also in residence on "Roman Brae" at this time was a young student named Alexander Smith, a future bishop. Yet another native of Banffshire, he had been sent home early from the Scots College in Rome because of health problems. He continued his studies at Greenock under the guidance of Mr Gordon and Bishop Scott, and on Candlemas Day, 2 February 1836, was the first priest ordained by the new Bishop Murdoch.

Mr Smith stayed on in Greenock for the next five years, and assisted Bishop Scott with the running of the Mission after the departure of Mr Gordon, who was transferred to St Andrew's, Glasgow in 1836. (Mr Gordon spent the next sixteen years in Glasgow, before returning to Greenock.)

The little church, bursting at the seams, had by 1837 undergone "a thorough repair . . . and a gallery, almost doubling the former accommodation (was) erected."[1] The church now seated approximately 700. Among other improvements, the windows were "tastefully stained".[1]

However, Bishop Scott was now burdened with a debt of £600.

In the newly-refurbished church there were two Masses on Sunday morning (referred to as "Public Service"), and instruction in the afternoon. There was Sunday school for children, who would not receive their First Communion until the age of twelve or more.

Catholics in Port Glasgow and Gourock, and even further afield, would walk into Greenock to attend Sunday Mass. One of the priests said Mass in Largs every six weeks.

The church renovations and the running expenses of the school were a huge drain on finances. Fewer than half the eligible children attended school, and then only for three or four years, most leaving aged 11 or 12 to go to work. Fees were 1½d to 3d (*1p to 1½p*) per week and a small grant was available from public funds to assist parents who could afford not as much. The teacher's salary, paid out of parish funds, was fixed at £50 a year, but could not always be paid in full or on time. (This state of affairs persisted until Catholic schools were taken into State control in 1918.)

* * *

In the Catholic Directories of the period, we find that Greenock and Paisley had the only two Catholic churches in the whole of

1. *Catholic Directory*, 1837, 1838.

Renfrewshire (the present-day Renfrew and Inverclyde Districts). In the whole of Scotland there were 81 priests and 66 churches, plus twenty Mass stations.

Besides Bishop Scott and Mr Smith, a third priest, Rev. Dr Peter Keenan, arrived at St Mary's about 1840. Born at Enniskillen, Co. Fermanagh, he had been brought up in Kirkcubrightshire, where his family had emigrated. Peter practised medicine in Glasgow for some years before going to Blairs to study for the priesthood. He seems to have followed an accelerated course, and after ordination he was sent for further studies in Paris, but was forced by illness to return to Scotland. In Greenock his skilled and devoted care of the sick gained him the affection and gratitude of Catholics and Protestants alike, and he was universally mourned at his tragically early death. Attending victims of one of the frequent typhus outbreaks, he contracted the disease, and died on 8 August 1843. He was only 32.

CHAPTER SEVEN

What Was Life Like?

ACCORDING to the 1841 census the total population of Greenock had grown to 36,836. Of these 4,307 were listed as "Irish-born", which gives an idea of the number of Catholics. They were from all parts of Ireland, but the vast majority came from Donegal.

Being a Catholic in the 1840s was quite demanding. There were many fast days when only one full meal was allowed: all weekdays in Lent, Wednesdays and Fridays in Advent, twelve Ember Days, and the vigils of six major feasts. And, of course, every Friday was a day of abstinence when no meat could be eaten.

The *Catholic Directories* of the period include notes for "Conduct in the House of God":

> "Catholics, who believe in the Real Presence of Jesus Christ in the Holy Eucharist, cannot show too much respect to the Temple of God.
>
> Persons whilst in the Church should as much as possible avoid coughing, spitting, and all manner of noise; as nothing that is offensive to the eyes should be seen, and nothing that tends to disturb or distract the attention should be heard in the House of God.
>
> They should be clean in their persons, and modest in their dress and deportment. It is very disrespectful to present themselves in the House of God unshaved, or with unwashed face or

hands; their apparel, however humble and poor, should be decent and becoming.

They should never shew any mark of levity or irreverence by looking about them, but keep their eyes on the Altar or on the Priest.

Mothers should take care not to bring children under age who might be apt to disturb the congregation.

Catholics should take care not to turn their backs to the Altar at any time, but especially when the Blessed Sacrament is exposed.

It is a scandalous practice to look about or talk before the service is commenced, or after it is ended. All should retire without noise or bustle, and in an orderly and edifying manner."

We are certainly more relaxed in church nowadays, and may smile at the quaintness of these instructions, but perhaps they might remind us to do our best to preserve something of our forebears' deep reverence for the Blessed Sacrament.

* * *

Around this time all the parish ministers in Scotland wrote their contributions for the *New Statistical Account* which gives a fascinating picture of life in the mid-nineteenth century.

Greenock was no longer the cosy, semi-rural little town depicted in the *Old Statistical Account* of 1793.

There were now seven shipyards, providing 1,200 jobs. A carpenter in the yards earned 1 guinea (*£1.5p*) per week. He would work ten hours a day in summer, and from sunrise to sunset in winter.

The eleven sugar-houses employed 350 people in total. Men earned 16/- (*80p*), and boys 5/- (*25p*) per week.

The Greenock Pottery had 270 employees. Men were paid between 8/- and £1.4s. per week (*40p* to *£1.20p*), and women between 2/6 and 7/- (*25p* to *35p*).

Farm-workers' wages were between £6 and £8 per half year "with bed, board and washing".

They were hired at the twice-yearly Greenock Fair (July and November), which was also a "feeing market".

A big new cotton mill was planned, for which workers' houses were in the process of being built. It was expected to employ between 300 and 400 people, mainly females aged from 13 to 22, with some males over 16.

There were 31 "inns and taverns" as well as 275 "shops for retailing ale and spirituous liquors".

The first pawn shop in Greenock had opened in 1830.

Although "assaults and street robbery are of comparatively rare occurrence . . . theft and housebreaking, and depradations on property of various kinds are often practised with impunity in the town as well as in the suburbs . . . from the insufficiency of the police force". They were apparently not as effective as their predecessors in the old Town Watch, with their "nocturnal perambulations".

There were three (yes, three!) mail deliveries daily, and hourly omnibuses (horse-drawn, of course) to Port Glasgow and Gourock "from 10 a.m. till late". Transport to Paisley and Largs was now by steamboat instead of stage-coach.

The river was busy. The Rev. Patrick MacFarlane, writing for the *New Statistical Account* speaks poetically of "the broad expanse of water with the multitude of whitening sails which bedeck its surface".

The railway arrived in Greenock in 1841, hewn through solid rock by Irish navvies. The fare to Glasgow was under 2/- (*10p*), and the journey took one hour and ten minutes.

Since 1829 the principal streets of Greenock had been lit by gas, and the more prosperous citizens would have gas lighting in their homes.

Although the Shaws Water Works had opened in 1827, it did not make much difference to the living conditions of the ordinary people, as the water supply was mainly used for industry. Disease was still rife among the overcrowded, insanitary "back lands".

* * *

For the last years of his life Bishop Scott had been suffering more and more from chest trouble. He continued to travel for as long as he could, but it was becoming more difficult for him as he grew increasingly frail. In October 1845 he resigned full control of the Western District to Bishop Murdoch.

Thereafter Bishop Scott's health deteriorated rapidly although his mind remained as clear as ever. The end came peacefully at St Mary's on 4 December 1846. The bishop was aged 74, and during his forty years as priest and bishop in Glasgow and Greenock he had worked tirelessly to build up the church in the West of Scotland. "His building was not just in stone; he had given courage to clergy . . . he had brought order and discipline where there had been laxity and lack of interest."[1] He laid a solid foundation for the Church in his District on which his successors were able to build.

The funeral was held in Glasgow: "To his own chapel of St Andrew's they brought him home and there, with a pectoral cross of the great Bishop Hay on his breast, he lay in state under his own roof, while his people mourned."[2]

Through streets lined with crowds his body was taken for burial in St Mary's, Abercromby Street.

* * *

These were the years of potato famine in Ireland, and destitute and starving refugees were arriving in their thousands. This country simply could not cope with the numbers, and the poor immigrants were forced to live in dreadful conditions. It is recorded, for instance, that in Glasgow eight adults and seventeen children were living in a cellar measuring ten feet by ten.

Every boat-load brought a fresh outbreak of disease, despite the fact that an official was employed to inspect every incoming ship for fever cases, and send them back to Ireland. Epidemics of typhus (spread by lice) and cholera (due to contaminated water) were of frequent occurrence. Tuberculosis was common.

The typhus outbreak of 1847 was the worst ever.

In Glasgow the situation was horrific. The fever hospital was full and sufferers who were turned away simply lay down on the grassy area in front of the nearby church. The five priests of St Andrew's, tireless and fearless in attending the sick, were all laid low. William Gordon was at death's door for some weeks. (He who could have chosen to enjoy the huntin' fishin' and shootin' life of a Victorian Highland laird instead of labouring among the foetid slums of Glasgow and Greenock.)

Only the saintly Bishop Murdoch escaped infection, and he wore himself out spending the entire day till ten o'clock at night visiting the sick, after which he spent most of the night bringing the Sacraments to the poor souls lying at the church door. It is recorded that because of his deafness he lay down beside them on the wet grass to hear their confessions.

Not surprisingly, he had a breakdown, and needed a long period of rest to recover his health.

---

1. Rev. Roderick Macdonald, *Bishop Scott and the Western Highlands (Innes Review,* 1966).
2. James Darragh, *Bishop Andrew Scott.*

Conditions in Greenock were not very different.

Among the 353 fever victims in Greenock was Rev. Richard Sinnott, who, having spent most of his priestly life in Galloway, returned to his home town when Bishop Scott died, and for a few months until his own death was in charge of St Mary's.

The *Greenock Advertiser* of 24 August 1847 pays a handsome tribute: "The Rev. Richard Sinnott, M.D., Roman Catholic clergyman of this town, died on Friday morning of typhus fever, adding another to the long list of priests of that communion, who, throughout the country, have lately fallen victims to that scourge . . . His quiet unassuming manners gained him the respect of his flock and of the public. His remains were on Sunday afternoon taken for interment to Glasgow . . . The hearse was followed as far as Port Glasgow by about a dozen carriages, and an immense assemblage of the congregation on foot. The time chosen was inconvenient, causing confusion on the streets at the time of the various churches coming out. Dr Sinnott is the second priest who, within the last few years, had died in this town of fever, caught in the discharge of their duties — the other being the Rev. Dr Keenan. Both of these gentlemen held medical diplomas — a circumstance that rendered their services as eagerly sought for as they were willingly accorded. It is impossible to record without regret the sacrifice they have been called on to make to the demands of duty — a sacrifice offered in the squalid hovels of the poor and destitute, out of sight of the world, and thus worthy of honours higher than all the glory of the warrior."

Dr Richard Sinnott, the first known Greenock-born priest. ***Portrait: Scots College, Rome.***

Like his predecessor John Gordon, Dr Sinnott was only 54 years old.

It seems strange to us that the funeral was held on a Sunday, but no doubt this was to allow people to attend without losing a day's pay.

* * *

A short time before this Port Glasgow was detached from St Mary's to form a separate Mission. The first resident priest was Rev. John Carolan who arrived in January 1846, and "proved himself to be brave and self-sacrificing"[1] during the cholera epidemic of that year. He soon started collecting funds, and in 1854 the fine church of St John the Baptist was opened.

From 1849 the Greenock priests were relieved of responsibility for Largs, which was now to be served from Bute.

1. William Forrest MacArthur, *History of Port Glasgow.* (Quoted by Rev. B.J. Canning, *Irish-Born Secular Priests,* p37).

CHAPTER EIGHT

"Priest Danaher" and the "Angel Gabriel"

THE composition of the Church in the Greenock-Paisley-Glasgow region was now completely altered, to be predominantly Irish, as shown in Mr Gordon's report of 1834. The Scottish clergy were overwhelmed by the vast numbers now claiming their attention, and were barely able to cope. Successive bishops sent urgent pleas to Ireland for assistance.

Rev. James Danaher

Now Irish priests began to arrive on the flood-tide of immigration. One of them was James Danaher, a Limerick man who volunteered for the Western District of Scotland. He was ordained in Glasgow in June 1845, and a few months later was posted to Greenock. After the tragic death of Dr Sinnott he was in charge of the Mission.

During the next five years there continued to be a fairly brisk turnover of assistant priests, until in 1850 Mr

Danaher's younger brother Francis, was appointed to serve as his curate. "He laboured here for nearly two years with zeal and effect, introduced several devotions, and founded a library for the use of the congregation."[1]

By this time Catholics in Greenock numbered around 6000. The church and school accommodation were quite inadequate, and James Danaher very soon began to raise funds for a second church. He set up schools in other parts of the town. His obituary states that "before the close of 1850 no less than seven day and night schools were in full operation."[2]

Mr Danaher came into conflict with the town's Parochial Board who administered the free charity schools, where Catholic children came under pressure to abandon their Faith. To counteract the "Greenock proselytisers", in 1849 he rented a large building in the east end of the town, to serve as a "Ragged School", providing free education for 150 poor children.

* * *

In 1851 the Catholic Directory reported that there were now 100,000 Catholics in the Western District, Greenock having the largest congregation after St Andrew's in Glasgow. However, things were not rosy. There were many "heavy pecuniary embarrassments, and deplorable spiritual destitution".

The assistance of the Irish priests was much needed to cope with the ever-increasing numbers. However, tensions began to arise among the clergy as the more ebullient Irish temperament clashed with the dour, cautious Scots, with their tradition of keeping a low profile as far as Catholic practice was concerned. Certain of the newcomers began to criticise the "Hielan clique", as they called those who were running the Church in Scotland, and claiming that the needs of the Irish were not being met. Just as in New Testament times the apostles were accused of favouring Jewish converts over Greeks. Human nature doesn't change!

Tensions were also growing in other sections of society, as the community struggled to come to terms with the vast numbers of newcomers pouring in, resented by some of the "natives". Large numbers of Irish navvies were at that time employed in building the

1. *Catholic Directory*, 1876.
2. *Catholic Directory*, 1888.

new Victoria Harbour (opened in 1850), and other public works. The Irish quickly gained a reputation for hard drinking and pugnacity. Some of the locals were not far behind them. Conflict began to break out as rival gangs of young men roamed the streets, particularly after a Saturday night's drinking. Each side naturally blamed the other for starting trouble.

On the wider political stage, the condition of Ireland was to be the major concern right through the second half of the nineteenth century and beyond, as the Nationalist Movement grew in strength, and the question of Irish Home Rule came to dominate British politics, with passions running high on each side. Anti-Irish and anti-Catholic meetings and demonstrations were taking place throughout Scotland in the period 1851-1855.

This was the situation when the Angel Gabriel flew in and fanned the flames.

This colourful character was one John Sayers Orr, a local man who during a long absence from the town seems to have had experiences which turned him violently anti-Catholic. He returned early in 1850, armed with a silver bugle, which he blew to attract an audience, hence the nickname. John Donald, the author of *Old Greenock Characters* gives a description of him: "under medium height, his oval face, swarthy complexion, jet black hair and short beard indicating a southern origin . . . (with) the foreign cap, the short, braided, dark brown velvet jacket . . ."[1] A favourite stance was the steps of the Custom-house, where he made his inflammatory speeches against Catholics and Irish. Quoting an eye-witness, John Donald reports: "He had a great flow of words, but a rambling way of speaking, repeating the same thing time after time. He had no connected or reasoned discourse. He would point to a man in the crowd and say, 'That man's an Irishman, I know by his face!'"[1]

John Sayers Orr, the "Angel Gabriel".

1. John Donald, *Old Greenock Characters (Second Series)* p134.

He certainly had good entertainment value, and no doubt many in the town went to listen to him for a "terr". But his most ardent followers were young shipyard workers, who took to parading the streets in gangs, carrying the axes they used in their work, stopping people "with a demand that they should say 'To hell with the Pope', and the word 'peas', which Irishmen usually pronounce 'paize'"[1]

One of their victims, a coalman with a sense of humour, replied, "I'm an Orangeman, and so is my donkey."[1]

Tough Irish navvies did not submit tamely to such provocation, and brawls were frequent.

The fiery Mr Danaher was not the man to shirk a fight, and he encouraged his people to stand up for themselves. He was accused by the *Scottish Protestant* newspaper of giving a series of talks during the winter of 1850 "in the coarsest and most offensive language, compared with which, John Orr's declamatory addresses were as the limpid stream to the stagnant pool . . . Protestants in general, as compared with Roman Catholics, were held up as the most ignorant, the most immoral, intolerant and debased people on the face of the earth."[2]

Even allowing for some exaggeration, one has the impression that "priest Danaher" as the paper calls him, would not miss and hit the wall when his dander was up!

Perhaps unsurprisingly, on 12 July 1851 the church and priest's house were attacked by a mob, and all the windows smashed. In the same week Catholic houses in Gourock and Inverkip were attacked and vandalised.

The sorry business rumbled on, not without moments of farce, as when the *Scottish Protestant* alleged that "Two Protestants, proceeding peaceably on the road to Inverkip" were attacked and robbed by "a number of Papists". Subsequently "two of the villains were apprehended" and charged, on the strength of damning evidence: "On the person of one of them was found a pair of drawers, the property of their victim."

Meanwhile the "Angel Gabriel" continued "instigating tumults" for which he was charged with breach of the peace on more than one occasion. He was a familiar sight blowing his bugle, "whether marching down East Quay Lane followed by a motley crowd . . . or emitting clarion calls from the top of an omnibus."[1] From time to time he

1. Ibid.
2. *The Scottish Protestant*, 6 September, 1851.

took a trip on one of the river steamers "blowing his horn and gesticulating, to the great delight of idlers gathered round."[1]

The ordinary decent townsfolk were naturally outraged at what was going on. It is on record that prominent citizens such as Rev. Dr James McCulloch, and the Provost, Samuel Paterson publicly reprimanded Orr, and tried to stop his tirades. In this they showed no small measure of courage, when the "Angel" was surrounded by a crowd of supporters, including his axe-wielding "bodyguard".

John Donald says that Dr McCulloch even confronted the gangs terrorising the town, and tried to make them disperse.

Things were so bad that the army had to be called in to restore order and two companies of the 93rd Highlanders from Glasgow were quartered in the town for a time.

The "Angel Gabriel" took flight across the Atlantic, and things quietened down without his inflammatory presence.

* * *

A change of pesonnel at the "Roman Brae" was in order. In 1852 the Danaher brothers were removed to Glasgow, and for the next few years no more Irish priests were sent to Greenock. A new curate, Glasgow-born Rev. Andrew Black, was appointed, and in May the Rev. William Gordon was sent back to St Mary's as Rector.

The Danahers were very much esteemed by their own congregation. Young Francis was admired for his zeal and loved for his kindness. "He was gentlemanly in his deportment, steady in his friendships, edifying in his conduct, ever attentive to the duties of his ministry, and always accessible to the poor."[2] "The Catholics of Greenock bestowed upon him many substantial proofs of their regard."[2] He subsequently spent 21 years at St Mary's, Duntocher until his early death at the age of only 48.

James, nicknamed the "Star of the West" was, as we have seen, a bit of a firebrand in his younger days. He was a fervent Irish Nationalist and a powerful orator. "He spoke in defence of the rights of the Irish people with a power and eloquence which awoke the patriotism of his audiences."[3]

He spent many years at St Mary's, Hamilton, where he died in 1886. His funeral was attended by "Protestant clergymen, the Provost

1. John Donald, op. cit.
2. *Catholic Directory,* 1876.
3. *Glasgow Observer,* 20 November 1886.

and Sheriff, most of the Magistrates and Town Councillors . . . which showed . . . the good feeling which exists, thinks to him . . . between Catholics and Protestants in Hamilton."[1]

Perhaps he mellowed with age, having learned something from his experience in Greenock!

Strangely, his name is omitted from the plaque at the back of the church which bears the names of deceased Rectors and Parish Priests. Was he an embarrassment? Or was it a simple oversight, since he lived for 34 years after leaving St Mary's, outliving his successor William Gordon by six years?

* * *

Back in Greenock trouble continued to break out from time to time, coming to a head on the evening of 27 December 1852. St Patrick's Band held a concert in the Mechanics' Institute in Sir Michael Street to raise funds to pay for their instruments. "Prior to the hour of meeting, groups of rough-looking youths and boys gathered about the vicinity of the hall, and annoyed people passing into the concert by jeering, hooting, and uttering party cries, such as 'Down with the Pope'. Their attitude was threatening; but no actual personal attack was made. It was a wet evening, and heavy showers were said to have kept the lads in check."[2]

Later in the evening, however, a threatening mob gathered outside the hall, battling for hours with the police who tried to disperse them. Stones were thrown, shop windows were broken, looting took place. In a night of rioting several people were injured.

After this things quietened down a bit, although sporadic fighting still went on. Then in 1855 the "Angel Gabriel" appeared again. This time the authorities took decisive action, and he was soon arrested, charged with breach of the peace and sentenced to sixty days' imprisonment. His supporters went wild.

On the evening of Monday, 2 April, "as darkness fell a crowd of several hundreds of men and boys gathered in front of the Roman Catholic Chapel at the north-western corner of East Shaw Street and Bearhope Street . . . and about eight o'clock an organised attack was instituted. While the major part of the mob assailed the windows of the chapel with sticks and stones, several of the leaders, armed with

1. *Catholic Directory*, 1888.
2. John Donald, *Old Greenock Characters (Second Series)* p139.

heavy wooden beams, smashed the entrance gateway to pieces. The Rev. Father Gordon was sitting quietly reading when he heard the shouts of the crowd, the crash of breaking glass, and the thuds of the battering ram against the chapel gate. In great alarm he hurried to the window and was horrified to perceive an immense hostile gathering of people . . . The reverend gentleman immediately had the windows barricaded, and well it was that this was done, for the entire framework of the windows was destroyed, while the entrance door to the manse was broken to pieces and the frames on which it hung driven out of place."[1]

The rioters then turned their attention to the school and the schoolmaster's house, smashing the doors and windows. A children's night-school class was in progress, but at the first sign of trouble the teacher, James Glacken, hastily led them out the back way, and all got home safely, although the father of one of the children was seriously injured when he arrived to collect his son.

It took two hours for the police to arrive. Their numbers were quite inadequate to control such a mob, and several were badly hurt. Several ringleaders were subsequently arrested. The following day a crowd bearing a battering ram attacked the jail in Bank Street in an attempt to set John Orr free, but he had already been transferred to Paisley. They then marched to the east end of the town where they attacked with stones the house of Bailie Speirs, who had sentenced the "Angel". In the by-going they smashed the windows of the Catholic school in Cartsdyke.

The Town Council once again called in military assistance, and a force of marines and 100 men of the Lancashire Militia were sent in to keep the peace.

Only four of the rioters were brought to trial. They were sentenced to six months each.

* * *

John Orr now took to travelling, continuing his crusade around the country, in Edinburgh, Liverpool, Dundee, and Paisley. He was not always well received; in Paisley, for instance, he was mobbed out of town. People were getting tired of him. With no means of support except the charity of his friends, he was reduced to poverty, and his appearance became more and more shabby. "An old woman who . . .

1. Ibid p143.

saw him for the first time, asked an acquaintance: 'Wha's that man?' 'That's the Angel Gabriel, granny.' 'Is that him? Hech, puir man, he maun be in the pook.'"[1] (moulting)

He expressed a desire to go to the West Indies, and his faithful followers in Greenock raised the money for his fare. He sailed off to Barbados in November 1855. The colonial authorities didn't mess about: he was soon arrested on charges of creating an unlawful assembly, libel, and inciting to riot. He was sentenced to three years' hard labour and died of dysentery in the penal settlement, a sad, pathetic figure in the end.

1. John Donald, op. cit.

CHAPTER NINE

Rev. William Gordon, "Mild, Genial and Gentlemanly"

OUTWARDLY, Greenock hadn't changed much during Mr Gordon's sixteen-year absence, except that it was bigger and dirtier. However, the first years of his Rectorship were marred by the ugly atmosphere of sectarian violence, with rioting breaking out periodically. Sugarhouse workers were particularly notorious for faction fights. As usual, it was a loutish minority which made the whole community suffer.

Rev. William Gordon

Rev. William Gordon, then Senior Priest at St Andrew's in Glasgow, was seen by Bishop Murdoch as the one man who could calm the situation and restore harmony. "Mr Gordon's genuine piety and devotion to his duties, his talents, and his refined manners, made him generally popular in Glasgow ... His urbanity in his intercourse with those outside his own Church served materially to dissipate the anti-Catholic prejudices once so prevalent in Glasgow."[1]

These qualities were just what was needed in troubled Greenock. Besides, during his previous residence in the town he had been liked and respected by all classes and all religions. He had maintained a warm friendship with the Rev. Dr James McCulloch, minister of the West Parish Church in Nelson Street (now called St Luke's), whose clock is, or was in my young days, still known as "McCulloch's Clock". According to John Donald, whose fascinating book gives such a vivid and balanced account of the "Angel Gabriel" troubles, it was Dr McCulloch who approached Bishop Murdoch in Glasgow to request that Mr Gordon be sent back to Greenock.

"He referred to the influence for good which the curate had exercised, the esteem with which he was generally regarded, and expressed the conviction that, with Father Gordon acting on one side and himself on the other, the rioters would be brought to reason and the tumults stopped. The Doctor's request was granted, and Father Gordon returned to Greenock in May, 1852. The two clergymen were . . . excellent friends. They worked, apart or together, always in harmony, and, in accordance with their plan of campaign, passed along the streets, often arm in arm, holding genial discourse, at meal hours and other times when they were most likely to be observed. The effect was very gratifying: quiet soon reigned, and the soldiers returned to Glasgow."[2]

The reality perhaps was not quite so simple, and as we have seen it took several years before things simmered down, but there is no doubt that the example of these two good men was very powerful. They were not alone, of course. It would be misleading to imply that sweetness and light prevailed at every moment, but as has already been mentioned, cordial relations between the denominations has been a feature of the town's history, at any rate among the more sensible members of the community.

Years later, when reporting his death, the *Greenock Telegraph* gave Dean Gordon, (as he had by then become,) full credit for bringing about this state of affairs: "The good and kindly feeling that now exists between those of his own denomination and others, is in a great measure to be attributed to the manner in which the Dean conducted himself, and also to the influence which he brought to bear upon his flock. It may be fresh in the minds of many residents of Greenock

1. *Catholic Directory*, 1882.
2. John Donald, *Old Greenock Characters (Second Series)* p.136

that riots of a disgraceful kind took place amongst people belonging to the different religions, and it is well known that the mild, genial, and gentlemanly manner which Dean Gordon exhibited towards all classes tended in a marked and powerful degree to soften down and at last to eradicate all feelings of animosity."[1]

William Gordon was universally loved and respected for his manifest goodness. Writing as late as 1920, forty years after the priest's death, John Donald obviously still remembered him vividly, and gives a glimpse of him in his description of "Blind Dominick", an old busker from Donegal. "While his performances as a violinist were in some respects striking, they by no means suggested the genius of a Paganini." He had only one tune in his repertoire, "The Girl I left behind me". "The story goes that Dominick was one day sawing away at his favourite melody when the late genial Dean Gordon, of St Mary's, passed. Slipping a coin into the blind fiddler's hand, he said, smiling pleasantly (that pleasant smile so characteristic of the man, and still so well remembered): 'Hurry up, Dominick, or the girl you left behind you will soon be before you.'"[2]

The Dean was a notable preacher, much in demand for special occasions. He had a clear, powerful voice, delivering his sermons "with fluency, grace and animation".[3]

"A profound scholar and possessing talents of the highest order, Dean Gordon was always ready in debate, and was yet liberal and considerate towards those who consistently differed from him in matters of religion."[1] A very special man indeed.

He found time to publish editions of various devotional books, including a Vesper Book, and an edition of the works of Bishop Hay.

* * *

The Western District continued to suffer "pecuniary embarrassments". Rev. William Gordon was Procurator (i.e. treasurer) of the Mission, and head of the distribution committee of the District Fund, set up "to assist struggling Missions (and) to establish new Missions."[4]

In April 1852 a joint pastoral letter was issued by Bishop Murdoch and his coadjutor Bishop Smith (the same who had spent some

1. *Greenock Telegraph,* 16 December, 1880.
2. John Donald, *Old Greenock Characters,* p93.
3. *Catholic Directory,* 1882.
4. *Catholic Directory,* 1853.

time in Greenock as a student and a young priest). In tones of pained reproof they deplored the smallness of the contributions to the Fund. The collection in Greenock amounted to £24 — an improvement on the previous year when nothing had been contributed! The bishops asked that each wage-earner give 1/- (*5p*) per annum. But the following year they were again expressing their disappointment.[1]

Times were not easy for the bishops. With the Catholic population continuing to grow dramatically, new churches were urgently needed. The number of clergy was also growing thanks to the influx of Irish priests, but many of them needed financial assistance as their people could often not support them adequately. Schools were also expensive to maintain.

Although there were growing numbers of Catholics among the better-off business people, the vast majority were living in poverty.

The probable explanation for Greenock's low contributions to the District collections is to be found in the determined effort of Rev James Danaher to provide a second church for the town. Even if they were not all regular churchgoers, 6,000 Catholics obviously placed a great strain on St Mary's, which could comfortably seat around 700.

Before his departure Mr Danaher was able to announce that £800 had been gathered for the new church, and Mr Gordon continued the fundraising.

A large number of Greenock's Catholics lived in the "Wee Dublin" area of Cartsdyke and Ladyburn, and it was in this part of the town that Mr Gordon was able to purchase a disused Protestant (Old Light Antiburgher) church. This had originally been bought by the Caledonian Railway Company, who sold it on to Mr Gordon when they altered their plans. It was re-opened on 12 August 1855 as St Lawrence's. A school was opened two years later.

Both congregations continued to be served from St Mary's until 1859 when Rev. Michael Condon, an Irish priest, was appointed to take charge of St Lawrence's.

Mr Gordon was entrusted with the task of establishing the bounds of the two Missions, and Mr Condon disagreed with him quite bitterly over this. After a year of wrangling the boundary was fixed at William Street and Bank Street.

* * *

1. See *Catholic Directories*, 1853-1854.

Nowadays as we leave the church after Sunday Mass we see the familiar sight of someone holding a collection plate for the Society of St Vincent de Paul. The founder of the Society was Frederic Ozanam (1813-1853), who while studying law at the Sorbonne in Paris was struck by the appalling poverty he saw in the city. In 1833 he joined with five other students to form the Conference of Charity. They took as their patron St Vincent de Paul (1581-1661) who devoted his life to helping the poor. The Society soon spread, and is now a world-wide organisation.

At a meeting on 2 July 1855 the Society's Council-General approved the establishment of St Mary's SVDP Conference. The SVDP is the oldest of our current Parish organisations, with almost 150 years of service to the needy.

Mr Gordon also fostered the setting up of a branch of the Catholic Young Men's Society, which flourished for many years. At the inaugural meeting on 28 October 1855 "many young and middle-aged men came forward". In fact there were no fewer than 273 members on the books, each paying 1½d per week "for the support or relief of sick members of the Guild."[1]

* * *

A century and a half of tradition. SVDP Conference, 2001: Standing, l. to r: Pat O'Donnell, Bill Fitzharris, Gerry Nelis, Bill McLellan, Jim Deegan. Seated: Bridget Robertson, Margaret Kane. Missing: Brian Brown. ***Photograph by F. M. Dunlop***

1. CYMS Minute Book, St Mary' Archives.

By this time the usual complement of priests at St Mary's was three. Assistant priests still tended to come and go fairly quickly, with the exception of Rev. Charles Reid, who spent fourteen years here, from 1854 until 1868.

He was an Aberdonian, one of three brothers who became priests. He was one of the many who struggled on despite bouts of ill-health. After his time in Greenock he was given charge of the new Mission at Helensburgh, but his health eventually broke down completely and he was forced to retire, aged only 51. He spent the remainder of his life in Rothesay, helping the priest there when he could. and spending his time reading "history, literature, (and) physical sciences." One gets the impression of a quiet, scholarly man, "straightforward, even to bluntness", but "most kind, considerate, and charitable".[1]

* * *

In the summer of 1859 Mr Gordon accompanied Bishop Murdoch on a trip to Spain to attend to business connected with the Scots College in Valladolid. It took three months to settle the affairs of the College, and no doubt Mr Gordon enjoyed the revisiting his old student haunts. He loved Spain, and always spoke warmly of his years spent there.

As Senior Priest in Glasgow he had, of course, worked alongside Bishop Murdoch, and they remained close friends. The Bishop reposed great trust in him, and had the highest regard for his ability. In 1861 the coadjutor Bishop Smith died at the tragically young age of 48, and the Bishop Murdoch's first choice to replace him was William Gordon. However, "from too great diffidence in his own powers he declined the burden of the episcopacy."[2]

There is no doubt that he would have made a fine bishop, but the Western District's loss was Greenock's gain.

Mr Gordon now undertook an ambitious building programme. He acquired a prime site in Patrick Street, and work began on the new St Mary's.

The architect chosen was George Goldie of London, who designed several other churches in Scotland, all dedicated to Our Lady.[3]

1. *Catholic Directory,* 1887.
2. *Catholic Directory,* 1882.
3. These churches were: St Mary's, Abercromby Street, Glasgow (1842); Our Lady of the Angels, Mingary (1842); St Mary's, Lanark (1856-9), which later burned down; Our Lady's, Fetternear (1859).

St Mary's Church, Patrick Street, as originally planned. *The Builder*, 28 December 1861.

CHAPTER TEN

"One of the Finest Churches in Scotland"

AT LAST the great day dawned: 17 August 1862, Sunday within the Octave of the Assumption of Our Lady, "under whose powerful invocation this temple is dedicated to Almighty God";[1] the day of the solemn opening of the new church.

The blessing of the church was conducted in the morning by Mr Gordon and later in the day Pontifical High Mass was celebrated by Bishop John Murdoch, with the attendance of eight priests, including the Rev. Alexander Munro of Paisley, who was the guest preacher.

The description in the *Catholic Directory*, possibly written by Mr Gordon himself, gives an eye-witness impression of the day:

"Notwithstanding the high price of the tickets, the building was densely crowded in every part, when the procession, headed by cross-bearer and acolytes, emerged from the sacristy, and proceeded by the left aisle, and up the nave, to the High Altar . . . After the Gospel, the

The unusual Coat of Arms of Bishop Murdoch, who officiated at the opening of the new Church on 17 August,1862.

1. *Catholic Directory,* 1863.

Rev. Mr Munro delivered a most impressive discourse on 'sacrificial worship,' with special reference to the Catholic teaching and worship in the sacrifice of the Mass . . .

"At the conclusion, the reverend preacher, looking upon the magnificent building in which they were assembled, as a munificent gift of the Catholics of Greenock to their children, called on them to complete the good work, by handing it down to their remotest posterity perfectly free and untrammelled from incumbrances of any sort, as a truly noble monument of their piety and generosity.

"The music was Mozart's Mass, No.12, which was performed by the members of St Andrew's choir, Glasgow, who, under the able superintendence of the Rev. Alex. Reid, and aided by the Greenock choir, rendered the whole of this charming composition in a very creditable manner."[1]

The full text of the *Directory*'s account, with a detailed description of the church, is given in Appendix 3. The total cost was £6000, and our ancestors did indeed manage eventually to clear the debt on the church, "handing it down to their remotest posterity (*That's us, folks!*) perfectly free and untrammelled from incumbrances of any sort".

Numerous alterations have taken place over the years: the Lady Chapel was a later addition, on the site of the original sacristy. The

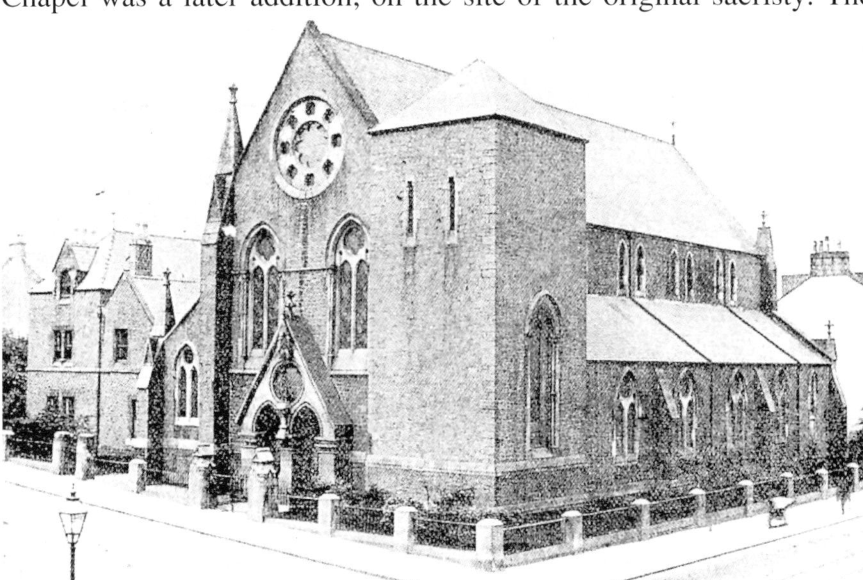

St Mary's, Patrick Street, in the late 19th century. Can you spot what's changed since then?

1. *Catholic Directory*, 1863.

High Altar was incomplete, the intention being to erect some form of canopy at a later date. The pulpit was a simple structure, to be replaced later with something more elaborate. There was no heating, of course, and the church was lit by "elegant gas fittings".

Old pictures of the exterior look a bit strange to our eyes because there was originally no door in the tower. The existing staircase to the organ loft was another later addition. When the church was first built, the loft was reached by a wooden spiral staircase on the left hand side of the church as you face the altar, and the space at the foot of the tower was occupied by the fine substantial baptismal font, with its inscription "Qui crediderit et baptizatus fuerit salvus erit" *(Whoever believes and is baptised will be saved).*

The tower itself was never completed because of the high cost. This gives the building its rather squat appearance. It was intended that the tower should be about twice as high, and house a belfry. Perhaps some day the Bells of St Mary's may yet ring out over Greenock.

The stained glass windows are a notable feature: St Andrew and St Patrick, with their borders of thistles and shamrocks, above the side altars (which were not built till later). But a gold star for those who can name the saints in the other six windows! From left to right they are: St Vincent de Paul, St Francis de Sales, Our Blessed Lady, St John, St Charles Borromeo, St Margaret.

A personal childhood memory is of Fr Molony in the pulpit for Devotions, with the evening sun streaming through St Patrick's window, falling on his sparse white hair, and giving him a beautiful coloured halo!

There is no doubt that the people of St Mary's were proud of their church, as indeed we still are! A later writer calls it "one of the finest churches in Scotland"[1], and who could argue?

Since St Lawrence's had been given a priest of its own, the hub of St Mary's Parish shifted west. As events turned out, the new church proved to be perfectly placed to serve both the old central area and the West End, where so many twenty-first century parishioners live. In the second half of the nineteenth century, however, the West End was just beginning to be built up, and still consisted mainly of large mansions of shipowners and sugar-house owners.

What of the old church on the "Roman Brae"? It was converted into a fine, spacious school, girls on the ground floor, boys on the

1. *Catholic Directory*, 1882.

upper. The girls were taught by Miss McDonnell, and the boys by Mr Sievewright.

The population of St Mary's continued to increase and multiply. During the 1860s immigration continued, as there was plenty of work available: new shipyards were opened, the new Albert Harbour was being constructed, and the excavated material was used to form the Esplanade. In 1862 there were 245 baptisms. It would not be long until the school accommodation was once again under strain.

* * *

In the new church there were three Sunday Masses, at eight, ten and twelve o'clock. Mass on weekdays was at nine. There was "Sunday School, with Catechetical Instruction, in the Church at three."[1]

It was a measure of the growing self-confidence of the Catholic community that they were able to erect such an imposing building in a prominent position in the town, and indeed, in Scotland as a whole, Catholic life was burgeoning. More Catholics were to be found now among the up and coming middle classes. Interesting reflections of this trend can be found in the advertisement pages of the *Directories* of the time:

"Neil Brown, Wine and Spirit Merchant, begs to inform Catholic Clergymen that he still continues to forward pure Spanish Wine to any part in Scotland, at 24/- (*£1.20*) per dozen, carefully packed with his own hand. Coal-nan Eeallan (*sic*) Whisky, allowed by competent judges to be the finest made in the West Highlands, will be supplied to Clergymen and Catholic Gentlemen at 16s 6d (*82½p*) per imperial gallon."[1]

Perhaps Mr Gordon placed an order to enhance the celebration dinner which no doubt was served in the new Rectory to the Bishop and visiting clergy!

"Robert Scott, Grocer, Tea, Wine and Spirit Merchant, Edinburgh", gives an idea of prices: tea was expensive at 3/4 (*22p*) per lb; coffee, 1/4 (*7p*) per lb; butter, 1/- (*5p*) per lb.[2]

In the 1860s, better-off Catholics could send their daughters to school at the Franciscan Convent school in Charlotte Street, Glasgow, where the fee of £4.10s. (*£4.50*) per quarter included "Board and General Education, and Plain and Ornamental Sewing". Washing

1. Catholic Directory, 1863.
2. Catholic Directory, 1860.

was 10/- (*50p*) extra. Day scholars would be taught "Reading, Writing, Arithmetic and Plain Sewing" for a fee of 7/6 (*37p*). Extras available were: French (£1), Italian (£1), Music (£1), Singing (10/-).

If you wished to send your eleven-year-old son to St Mary's College, Blairs, the fees were £30 per annum for "Board and Education". If he was a student for the priesthood you would pay for his board the first year only. You would have to supply him with "a new suit of Black Clothes, consisting of Surtout Coat, Waistcoat and Trousers, for Sunday" and "a new suit of strong Dark-coloured Clothes for daily wear."[1]

1. Catholic Directory, 1860.

CHAPTER ELEVEN

Changing Times

IN AUGUST 1867 a newly-ordained young curate was sent to St Mary's. Rev. Alexander Taylor was the last of the "Banff Brigade" to serve here. Born like so many priests before him in the Enzie of Banffshire, he had studied at the Propaganda Fide College in Rome, and was ordained in the Lateran Basilica on 18 July. From the start he and Mr Gordon seem to have become good friends, both being from the same part of the country, and both being of pleasant, affable temperament. The younger priest looked up to his Rector as a model of priesthood, and was glad to follow his guidance. Between the two of them, they spanned the second half of the nineteenth century at St Mary's.

After only a few months Mr Taylor was assigned to a temporary teaching post at Blairs College, but after a year or so he was sent back to Greenock, where he was to remain until his death in 1905. He was the longest-serving priest ever at St Mary's, where "his strong devotion to duty and his large-heartedness won the affection of his people".[1]

* * *

The year after Mr Taylor's arrival sufficient funds were available to make some additions to the church: "Two new side Altars — the one dedicated to St Andrew, the other to St Patrick — have been

1. *Greenock Telegraph*, 6 January 1905.

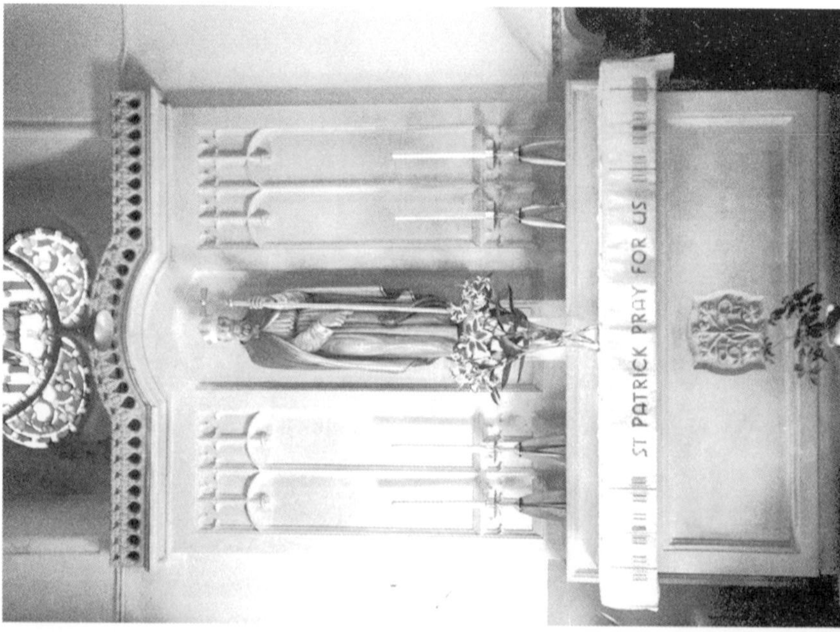

Photograph by F. M. Dunlop.

THEN . . . AND NOW.

erected in this Church. They are both very beautiful, and quite in harmony with the building. The drawings of them were given by Mr Goldie, the architect of the Church."[1] Mr Gordon was obviously quite proud of them!

It was a surprise to discover that what is now the Sacred Heart Altar was originally dedicated to St Andrew, although, of course, the stained glass window above shows the saint. Devotion to the Sacred Heart of Jesus had been increasing steadily since the Feast was established by Pius IX in 1856. The Sacred Heart Confraternity was founded in 1873 by the Vincentian Fathers, and popularised by them as they conducted Parish Missions. The Confraternity flourished in St Mary's for many years. Pope Leo XIII encouraged this devotion, and consecrated the world to the Sacred Heart of Jesus in 1899.

By that time, too, most of the congregation were Irish or of Irish descent, with less reason to honour St Andrew. So his altar was re-dedicated to the Sacred Heart, probably around the turn of the century.

* * *

On a wider stage, things were happening. The restoration of the Hierarchy had taken place in England, and there was some debate on whether the time was ripe for a restoration in Scotland also. The Vicars Apostolic feared it might stir up anti-Catholic feeling, but Archbishop Manning of Westminster, sent by Rome to report on the situation, took a different view: "In the face of Protestant public opinion in Scotland the establishment of the hierarchy, prudently carried out, would not bring any danger of opposition. The Presbyterians nowadays concede to others full freedom of conscience and religious observance ... The change would not be noticed by outsiders."[2]

Before this took place there were some problems to be ironed out. Discontent persisted among some of the Irish clergy who felt they had not received fair treatment from Bishop Murdoch, and his successor, Bishop Gray. In an attempt to ease the situation an Irishman, Rev James Lynch, was appointed by Rome as coadjutor Bishop. However, he and Bishop Gray found it impossible to work together.

1. *Catholic Directory*, 1869.
2. Rev. James Walsh, *Archbishop Manning's Visitation of the Western District of Scotland in 1867. (Innes Review, Spring 1967.)*

After less than three years he returned to Ireland, and the ailing Bishop Gray retired, resigning the Vicariate to Archbishop Charles Eyre, a neutral Englishman, appointed in 1869 as Apostolic Administrator for the Western District, who "would be able to pour oil on the troubled waters of the Clyde".[1] He also held the rank of Apostolic Delegate to Scotland, with the long-term remit of preparing for the Restoration of the Hierarchy.

The new Archbishop "was a man of commanding presence, physically, intellectually and spiritually. He refused to pay any heed to the petty national jealousies which had divided his flock."[2]

With great efficiency and energy he set about reorganising the Western District, working hard to unify clergy and people, and tightening up administration.

One of his first acts was to divide the Western District into deaneries. Locally, St Peter's Deanery consisted of St Mary's, St Lawrence's, Port Glasgow, Houston, Alexandria, Dumbarton, Helensburgh, Dunoon, Rothesay, Largs and Campbeltown, all of which places had resident priests by now. Rev. William Gordon was chosen as Dean, and as such had oversight of the local clergy.

Deanery priests were required to meet in conference three times a year for a formal discussion of topics set by the Archbishop. A few examples of these show some of the concerns of the time:

• What was the correct attitude to societies such as Freemasons? (6 April, 1875)[3]

• On the problem of drunkenness: was it better to advocate temperance or total abstinence? (21 Sept 1875)[3]

• On the pastoral care of young people: should dancing be encouraged or not? (May 1877)[3]

There were also a number of discussions on Liturgy.

Each priest had to submit his thoughts in writing, and the minutes of the meeting were to be forwarded to Glasgow. "Great care should be taken that the Conferences do not degenerate into mere convivial meetings."[4] No messing with this Archbishop!

However, there was a social side, which no doubt facilitated what we would nowadays call "bonding". "The cost of the Conference dinner is to be 3s. (*15p*), and each member of the Conference has to contribute that sum towards it whether he be absent or present."[4]

1. Peter F. Anson, *Underground Catholicism in Scotland,* p319.
2. Mgr David McRoberts, quoted by Peter F. Anson, op. cit. p320.
3. Minute Book of Deanery Meetings, St Mary's Archives.
4. Archbishop's Regulations, 1869.

After all their serious deliberations, one hopes that the 3/- per head stretched far enough to include a few bottles of Neil Brown's "pure Spanish wine"!

* * *

The year 1872 saw the passing of the Education (Scotland) Act which made school attendance compulsory between the ages of five and thirteen, and set up School Boards which allocated grants from the local rates.

The position of Catholic schools was unchanged in theory, but "in practice they had to carry a heavier burden than before. Now they were obliged to contribute to local rates, to maintain and build new public schools . . . Catholics did not have a share in any of the public funds derived from these rates."[1]

Unhappy with the character of compulsory religious education in the new State schools, Catholics opted to pay for their own, and made heroic efforts to do so.

In July 1873 the new Burgh School Board carried out a survey of all the schools in Greenock. It was reported that St Mary's School in the old converted church in East Shaw Street consisted of two school-rooms and one smaller class-room. There were 555 children on the roll, the average daily attendance for the past month being 455. There were thirty part-time pupils, who were probably employed in factories or other work.

In the Elementary Division all 555 pupils were being taught Reading, but only 357 were learning Writing and Arithmetic, which seems rather strange.

In the Advanced Division the numbers were: English Grammar and Geography, 79; History 62; Composition 55.

All 555 pupils had Singing lessons; 62 had Drawing, and Needlework was being taught to 100 girls. All pupils had "two and a half hours weekly in Bible Lesson and Catechism."[2]

"The books in use are those issued by the Commissioners of National Education, Ireland."[2]

Fees still ranged from 1d to 3d per week.

The staff of the school consisted of the Head Master, Archibald McDonald, the Head Mistress, Miss Ann McDonnell, "both

1. Peter F. Anson, op. cit. p326.
2. *Report on School Accommodation, July 1873,* Greenock School Board Minute Book.

certificated, one female assistant, four male and four female pupil teachers."[1]

"There are separate water closets for the male and female pupils, but no playground, otherwise the school accommodation is good."[1]

Although they received no funding from local Councils, Catholic schools did receive a small Government grant, part of which helped to pay the teachers' salaries. The level of grant was dependent on results, and it could be withheld if the work of the school did not come up to standard. As can be imagined, no effort was spared to make a good impression on H.M. Inspector.

"The story is told that, in order to secure the highest payment, some teachers resorted to a simple trick. When, in the presence of the Inspector, the class teacher questioned his class on a topic, all the children's hands went up. The teacher asked a pupil for the answer, received the correct response and, thereby impressed the Inspector that excellent teaching had been going on. What the Inspector failed to notice was that the teacher only asked questions of those pupils whose RIGHT hands were raised . . . Those who were ignorant simply raised their LEFT hands and were, of course, ignored by the teacher!"[2] (It is not, of course, suggested that St Mary's teachers employed such subterfuge!)

Dean Gordon took great care and delight in instructing children, "To them especially he was full of life and fatherly tenderness, earnest in implanting in their young minds not only a love of their religion, but an intelligent knowledge of it also."[3]

The Dean was elected to Greenock Burgh School Board, where he used all his tact to preserve good relations. "Sitting in council with Protestants, he never asserted his own religious views, but seemed to make it his study to say nothing that could by any possibility be misconstrued, or that could possibly give offence."[4]

He managed to do this without being the least bit mealy-mouthed. "In the statement of his convictions he was always explicit and uncompromising. . . No person who knew him and had conversed with him on religious topics was ever left in the least doubt as to his candid opinion on those subjects. At the same time, I believe that few priests of his time, if any, had a wider circle of acquaintances outside

1. *Report on School Accommodation, July 1873,* Greenock School Board Minute Book.
2. Thomas P. F. Murray, *St Columba's High School Golden Jubilee* booklet.
3. Funeral oration by Bishop Angus Macdonald, *Greenock Telegraph,* 23 December 1880.
4. *Greenock Telegraph,* 16 December 1880.

the Catholic communion; and none enjoyed a larger share of their esteem and confidence."[1]

* * *

It was a severe blow when the Dean was suddenly laid low by illness in 1873. "He had, in the pulpit, with even more than his usual eloquence, been warning his flock against the vice of intemperance,"[2] when he suffered a stroke.

Father Taylor was a tower of strength at this time, and during the next few years, when more and more of the burden of responsibility fell on him, for although the Dean recovered, he was never as robust as formerly, and his health gradually deteriorated from now on.

The young curate, Rev. Alexander Taylor

1. *Greenock Telegraph,* 16 December 1880.
2. Funeral oration by Bishop Angus Macdonald, *Greenock Telegraph,* 23 December 1880.

CHAPTER TWELVE

"Education, Education, Education"

THE NEXT few years saw some important developments in education. In 1874 at the invitation of Rev. Michael Condon, Franciscan Sisters of the Immaculate Conception came from Glasgow to take charge of St Lawrence's School. Fr Condon bought for them the imposing Georgian house in Bank Street, which still stands, recognisable by its elegant double entrance staircase. This was the original Bank House which gave the street its name. (It is now Jericho House.) Here the Sisters soon opened a private school — "a middle-class school for day scholars."[1] Hitherto "middle-class" parents sent their children to local non-Catholic private schools, or for a Catholic education further afield, for instance to St Aloysius', or Charlotte Street Convent.

There were five Sisters in the original community, under their Superior, Mother Mary Baptist.

One of the pupils at the Convent in those early days was a little boy called Tommy Taylor, who served as an altar boy in the Sisters' Chapel. He was to become the renowned Mgr Thomas Taylor, who founded the Carfin Grotto and was one of the most distinguished churchmen of his generation. He died in 1963, just a fortnight short of his ninetieth birthday.

At St Mary's, the school in the converted church in East Shaw Street had become too small, and a grand project was undertaken to demolish it and replace it with a brand new school. Archbishop Eyre

1. *The Catholic Church in Greenock*, 1880.

was invited to lay the foundation stone on Saturday 13 October 1877.

A later writer gives such a vivid account of the proceedings that we could almost imagine we were present. It is worth quoting at some length:

"Punctually at 3.30 p.m., a procession of full 2000 men started from St Mary's Church. It was headed by the Benefit Society, with their flute band, followed by the Young Men's Society, the Congregational Society with their brass band and banners, and the Building Committee. His Grace, the Most Rev. Dr Eyre, and Dean Gordon closed the procession (which) wended its way along Patrick Street, Ardgowan Street, Nelson Street, and East Shaw Street.

"Arriving at the new building, his Grace was received with round upon round of cheers. Here was gathered an assemblage of nearly 10,000 spectators, occupying every coign of vantage from the ground to the chimney tops.

"Dean Gordon opened the proceedings by introducing the Archbishop to the assembled people. He then presented him with a

Above: The "splendid Gothic structure" of St Mary's School, East Shaw Street. Built on the site of the original Church — it was opened on 2 October, 1878.

Right: The same view in 2001.
Photograph by F. M. Dunlop

handsome silver trowel, the work of Mr Smith, Silversmith, West Blackhall Street.

"After having blessed and declared the foundation stone well and truly laid, the officiating prelate addressed those gathered around. His first words, he said, must be words of congratulations and encouragement to Dean Gordon and Father Taylor. He went on to maintain the right of parents to bring up their children in the religious tenets which they themselves professed — insisting particularly on the rights of Catholic parents. On the other hand, children, too, had their rights. On the day of their baptism they had acquired the right to be instructed in the faith — to be taught how to walk in that faith.

"When his Grace ended, ringing cheers were given for him and for the occupants of the platform, amongst whom were some of the leading Protestant citizens of the town. Throughout the whole ceremony Father Taylor acted as master of ceremonies, and it is a matter of the highest credit to him that, notwithstanding the vast numbers who were present, he carried out every detail of the function without the slightest hitch . . . At the conclusion of the ceremony, Dean Gordon entertained His Grace and a large number of guests to luncheon in the Tontine Hotel."[1] (This was the old Tontine in Cathcart Street.)

* * *

As 1878 dawned, with the Catholic population of Scotland now standing at 332,600, the country was preparing to graduate from the status of a Mission Territory to a country with normal Church government. Before the preparations were complete Pope Pius IX died, and the first act of the new Pope Leo XIII, on 4 March, the very day of his coronation, was to restore the Scottish Hierarchy. The three Vicariates were abolished, and six dioceses established. Rt Rev. Charles Eyre became the first Archbishop of Glasgow since the death of James Beaton two hundred and seventy years before. That notable convert, the Third Marquess of Bute, presented jewelled mitres to all the Scottish bishops.

Greenock was part of the new Archdiocese of Glasgow.

(Although Archbishop Manning had thought that "the change would not be noticed by outsiders", sporadic protest riots took place throughout the country.)

The first Archdiocesan synod was held in St Andrew's Cathedral,

1. Bazaar Handbook, 1897.

Glasgow, on 19 October 1881, at which around 110 of the clergy were present, along with the Archbishop. It was reported that Glasgow Archdiocese, with 215,732 souls and 134 priests, "contains more Catholics than all the other five dioceses combined, and its clergy compose the exact half of the whole clergy of the country."[1]

* * *

Later that same year the Archbishop was welcomed back to Greenock to perform the opening ceremony at the new St Mary's School. "Old age and infirmities had come upon Dean Gordon, but, thanks to the untiring energy of Father Taylor and his committee, the splendid Gothic structure in East Shaw Street stood ready for occupation on Tuesday, 2nd October, 1878."[2]

Fortunately, the weather was favourable once again, as nearly 1,000 children gathered for Mass in the church before marching from Patrick Street to their new school, where "the boys, with their parents and friends, assembled in one of the large halls of the schools, whilst the girls gathered in another."[2] Along with the Archbishop were the now frail Dean Gordon, with his curates Fathers Taylor and Graham, plus no fewer than twelve visiting priests, and Mr Ingram, the architect of the "splendid Gothic structure."

It is recorded that "Mrs McInally presided at the harmonium, and Mr Gillies at the piano, accompanied by Mr Brockbank on the cornet."[2]

After the ceremony of blessing, the children presented the Archbishop with "a beautiful silver inkstand, a bouquet of flowers, and an address of welcome and thanks". The Archbishop made a gracious speech of thanks, in which he remarked that "the flowers were fresh and beautiful like the children themselves."[2]

Father Taylor was then presented with "a very handsome writing desk, a bouquet of flowers", and an address in which he was thanked for "his unwearied kindness towards teachers and children", and his "labours towards the erection of their schools".[2]

In his reply Father Taylor paid gracious tribute to "the interest which Dean Gordon had taken in the work",[2] although illness had prevented him from being actively involved. The proceedings were closed by the Dean calling for three cheers for the Archbishop.

1. *Catholic Directory*, 1882.
2. Bazaar Handbook, 1897.

That was not the end of the celebrations on this momentous day. In the evening a large number returned to the school, where "the members of St Mary's Parish held a soiree and concert. His Grace, the Archbishop, presided. He was supported on the platform by the Right Rev. Angus McDonald, Bishop of Argyll and the Isles."[1] Dean Gordon was well enough to attend, and one of the town's ministers, the Rev. Mr Fullarton, was also present.

"The choir opened the proceedings with an excellent rendering of the Gloria from Mozart's 12th Mass."[1] (This was the Mass which had been sung at the opening of the church in Patrick Street.)

In his opening remarks the Archbishop gave "unstinted praise . . . to Fathers Gordon and Taylor for their magnificent efforts in building a monument which attested to all the world that religion and education could never be divorced. Catholics could never allow their children to be trained where religious influences did not prevail, where their hearts and their consciences would not be formed along with their minds.

"During an interval in the programme a number of prominent gentlemen of the congregation partook of a cake and wine banquet purveyed by Mr Sieger."[1] There were speeches and toasts, before the second half of the concert took place "with the greatest satisfaction".[1] There is no mention of prominent ladies of the congregation. No doubt they were dutifully handing round the cake and wine!

The new school was placed in the care of the Franciscan Sisters. The first headmistress was Sister Mary Angela, and her assistant was Sister Mary Nativity. Mr Fagan was in charge of the boys.

Although it is reported that close on 1,000 children attended the opening of the new school, the average daily attendance for that year was only 517. No doubt some pre- and post- school-age children would be taken along, but at this period, despite the Education Act, regular school attendance was still by no means universal.

* * *

Dean Gordon's health continued to decline to the point where he was no longer able to celebrate Mass. This must have caused him great distress. In fact he said Mass for the last time on Sunday 20 July 1879, and thereafter was more or less confined to the house, where he was cared for by his devoted housekeeper, Miss Campbell.

1. Bazaar Handbook, 1897.

A year later he made a great effort to attend the opening of the new "chapel-school" in Gourock. Father Taylor, who had been in charge of the project, was the chief celebrant at High Mass in the "pretty little church", as the *Greenock Telegraph* calls it. Gourock continued to be served from St Mary's until in 1896 it became a separate Mission, dedicated to St Ninian.

This was Dean Gordon's last public appearance. By the end of the year he was very ill, and he died peacefully on the afternoon of Wednesday, 15 December, 1880, just a few weeks short of his 73rd birthday. By coincidence, it was the anniversary of the death of his great friend, Bishop John Murdoch.

He had asked to be buried "in St Mary's, among my own people, that they may pray for me",[1] and so he was laid to rest in the vault in front of the Sanctuary, after a Requiem celebrated in the presence of Archbishop Eyre and Bishop Macdonald of Argyll and the Isles who preached at the end of the Mass. No fewer than 57 priests were present, including the Dean's two nephews. "The number of priests present was probably greater than on any similar occasion in Scotland."[2] The packed congregation included many prominent Protestants, whom the Dean had counted among his friends.

Dean William Gordon was only one of our many "great and noble priests", whose names, according to Bishop Macdonald, "will be held in benediction, and will be embalmed in the grateful remembrance of generations to come".[1]

1. Funeral Oration by Bishop Angus Macdonald, *Greenock Telegraph,* 23 December 1880.
2. *Catholic Directory,* 1882.

CHAPTER THIRTEEN

Rev. Alexander Taylor "An Ideal Priest"

IT WAS with great satisfaction that the people of St Mary's heard news of the appointment of the much-loved Father Alexander Taylor as successor to Dean Gordon. He had in fact been responsible for running the parish for several years, and his outstanding qualities were well known. "An able preacher and an erudite scholar, he was an ideal priest."[1]

Like his predecessor, Fr Taylor was "of a genial and good-natured disposition",[2] and shared his talent for making friends. "He was of very scholarly attainments, and a splendid linguist, speaking French, Italian, and Spanish with great fluency, and as a pulpit orator he ranked high. Possessing a fine presence, having a splendid voice, and using choice but simple language, he was ever heard with pleasure. His discourses were always prepared with commendable care, and never failed to convey a

Rev. Alexander Taylor

1. *Greenock Telegraph*, 6 January 1905.
2. *Catholic Herald* , January 1905

vast amount of instruction within a small compass. He possessed a charming manner, and it has been remarked that all the clergymen who had been his curates remained his fast friends, and were always glad of an opportunity to visit him."[1]

He had a fine singing voice, and was very fond of music. He took a great interest in St Mary's choir, which at that period "was always admitted to be the finest in Greenock".[1]

"Everything affecting the members of the congregation was of concern to him, and he was never happier than when amongst them. Their social reunions were a source of keen delight to him, and it was a pleasure to see him beam on them from the chair on such occasions."[1]

* * *

During the nineteenth century the Temperance Movement flourished throughout the country, attempting to combat the very prevalent abuse of alcohol. Cardinal Manning visited St Mary's on 1 June 1881 to inaugurate the League of the Cross, a temperance society which he had founded in London ten years before. By 1885 the League had around three hundred members in St Mary's, and was to last well into the Twentieth Century.[2]

An important event about this time was the arrival in the town of the Little Sisters of the Poor. Already established in Glasgow, they sought permission from Archbishop Eyre to open a Home for the Aged Poor in Greenock. Given the poverty of their congregations, the local priests had serious misgivings, fearing that it would be placing an unfair burden on the people to expect them to support a new foundation. However, Fr Taylor and Canon Condon of St Lawrence's visited the Little Sisters' establishment in Glasgow and were so impressed by what they saw that their doubts vanished. Thereafter both became enthusiastic supporters of the Sisters, who in January 1884 began the search for suitable premises in Greenock.

Sheriff Harvey Smith lived in an imposing villa, No. 44 Union Street, at the corner of Campbell Street. He had also bought the house next door (No. 46), to ensure that he would not be troubled by awkward neighbours! Next door to this again was another large villa (No. 48), which the Sisters were able to rent from the Railway

1. *Catholic Herald*, January 1905.
2. Cf. Rev B.J. Canning, *Diocese of Paisley*, p115.

Company who owned it. Great was their disappointment when they learned that the existing tenants were not due to leave until May. However, Providence smiled on the enterprise, and Sheriff Smith agreed to lease the middle villa, No. 46, to Mr Ward, a Glasgow benefactor of the Sisters.

On 19 February five Sisters moved into a house which was dirty, cold and damp, and in need of urgent repairs, after lying empty for three years. Their first task was to clean up the house and make it habitable.

Within the week they welcomed their first resident. When he came to bless the house, Fr Taylor told them of eighty-year-old Helen McKay, living in great poverty in a miserable attic. By the summer the Sisters were caring for thirty needy old people, rising to sixty by October.

In May they duly took possession of No. 48, and a few years later in 1888, they were able to take over the third house, No. 44 at the corner, when Sheriff Smith moved out of town. "We like this peaceful site, just at the end of the town, with its magnificent views over the Clyde to the hills beyond."[1]

The Sisters became a familiar sight, going their rounds collecting donations with their pony and cart, a gift from a Mr Hagan and his friends.

From the beginning, the Sisters were overwhelmed by the generosity of the local people. One young sister "could not express her emotion at seeing the poor workmen giving so generously, and sometimes depriving themselves to do so."[1]

Local business people also were generous. "The first Christmas morning a baker sent a basket of hot rolls with a fine cross traced on each one, for the old people."[1] On New Year's Day, 1885, "a baker sent a basket of lovely cakes for the aged . . . The railway sent us six rabbits and six hares."[1]

Reading of those early days one is reminded of stories of Don Bosco, and how he and his "family" were miraculously provided for.

"We prayed for potatoes as we had little left and they were our chief means of subsistence. . . There was a ring at the door, and on the doorstep was a servant from one of the houses bringing a huge sack of potatoes from his mistress."[1]

"We could not pay the gas bill amounting to £2.19/-. A lady sent us £2.10/-, almost the exact sum."[1]

1. *Foundation Book*, quoted by Rev. Bernard J. Canning: *Instruments of His Work* (Centenary Brochure)

The Little Sisters attribute all to the intercession of their beloved St Joseph.

* * *

"On 21st August, 1887, the Sunday within the Octave of the Assumption, the congregation celebrated the silver jubilee of the opening of St Mary's."[1] Pontifical High Mass was celebrated by Archbishop Eyre, and the preacher was Mgr Munro, who had preached at the opening of the church twenty five years previously. It is reported that the church was crowded for the occasion, "whilst a special train brought numerous friends from Glasgow and the surrounding districts".[1]

1887 is the date on the fine atmospheric painting of St Mary's by the Greenock artist Patrick Downie. My guess is that it was commissioned to celebrate the Silver Jubilee. The painting is reproduced at the front of this book.

In passing we can record as an interesting footnote, that in this same year a small sailing vessel named "Nell" was launched at Greenock. She was destined for service as a Mission Vessel, transporting a priest around the Western Isles. She is now in the Marine Docks at Dover.

Big changes were now taking place in the church building, which

The earliest known photograph of the Church interior, taken soon after the installation of the new High Altar in 1890. Note the temporary pulpit, and the "elegant gas fittings" upstanding under the side arches. In 1914 the original benches were replaced and the Lady Chapel built, on the left of the picture.

1. *Catholicity in Greenock*, p17.

was closed for two months in 1890 while a magnificent new High Altar was erected by Messrs Pugin & Pugin. Costing almost £600, it was the gift of Miss Ellen O'Brien, in memory of her parents. The whole church was redecorated, and reopened on Sunday 20 October, with High Mass at which the celebrant was Canon Maguire V.G. (Vicar General of the Archdiocese). (A newspaper misprint awarded him the V.C.!) Archbishop Eyre "preached a most impressive sermon, which was listened to with rapt attention by the large congregation."[1]

Another happy event took place two years later, as parishioners celebrated with Father Taylor the Silver Jubilee of his priesthood. On 31 October 1892 a grand concert was held in the Temperance Institute at which he was presented with a purse of 110 sovereigns, a very large sum at the time, and an indication of the regard in which he was held. Among the large gathering were many visiting priest-friends, including several who had served as curates in St Mary's during the previous twenty-five years.

* * *

Father Taylor's busy life continued. He was chaplain to the Little Sisters, and to the Prison, which was at that time situated in Nelson Street. It was noted that he made almost daily visits to the Infirmary, with its fever wards: "Disease had no terror for him."[2] He was President of the League of the Cross, and took a close interest in the other Parish organisations, such as the Young Men's Society and the Society of St Vincent de Paul.

The Sick Call Book[3] for these years gives a glimpse of the work of the priests, taking the year 1891 as a typical example:

January	44 sick calls, 13 of whom died (There were six calls in one day on 13 Jan. All received the Sacrament of Extreme Unction).
February	36 calls
July	23 calls
October	36 calls, 10 of whom died
November	76 calls, 15 died On the 13th of the month Fr De Monti was on duty. He was called out six times that day.

1. Ibid, p18.
2. Rev. W. P. O'Brien, quoted in *The Catholic Herald* (?), January 1905.
3. St Mary's Archives.

Each year in the month of May all the priests went to Smithston Poorhouse on a Saturday night to hear Confessions. One of them returned the following morning to give Communion, enabling the inmates to fulfil their Easter Duties. In those days it was usual to receive Holy Communion only once or twice a year.

In 1891 there were 59 Communions at the Poorhouse.

The winter of 1896-7 took a severe toll. In 1897 the priests answered 59 sick calls in February; 19 died. In March the total was 41, 22 of whom died.

In May that year Father Taylor took a trip to Dunoon to administer the Sacraments to the priest there who was ill.

* * *

Education was one of Father Taylor's main concerns. He was first elected to the Burgh School Board in 1876, and "remained, except for one term when he did not seek re-election, a member till the time of his death. He was greatly respected by the members of that body, and on more than one occasion he headed the poll at the elections."[1]

The school in East Shaw Street was once again impossibly overcrowded, the average attendance having risen to around 851 in 1892. The First Standard boys, girls and infants were transferred to a rented hall in Sir Michael Street, the headquarters of the Irish Democratic League. This was not very satisfactory as it was "a dark and dingy hovel", according to a later headmaster, Henry J. Kilpatrick. And still the numbers continued to grow. For the year ending 31 October 1895 the average daily attendance was 952. (440 infants compared with 268 three years previously.) H.M. Inspector of Schools insisted that new accommodation must be provided, but the Parish was already struggling under a large burden of debt, and no assistance was available to Catholic schools from public funds.

Something had to be done urgently, and an ambitious project was undertaken. At a Parish meeting, it was decided to organise a Bazaar, and an executive committee was formed consisting of 17 gentlemen of the Parish, plus Father Taylor (Treasurer) and his three curates, Fathers Lynch, Fleming and Mann.

The President of the Committee was Bailie Robert Cook, the first Catholic to be elected to the Town Council.

The "Bazaar and Fancy Fair" ran from Thursday 9th to Saturday

1. *Catholic Herald*, January 1905.

11th December 1897. It was a magnificent affair, with eight stalls, plus a lucky dip, billed as the "Fish Pond and Fairy Well"! These were staffed by well over 150 ladies and girls of the Parish and friends. There was also a Refreshment Stall providing "Dinners, Luncheons and Teas, at Moderate Charges."

Miss O'Brien, the donor of the new Altar, was in charge of Stall No.1.

It was a measure of the abiding influence of the beloved Dean Gordon, that seventeen years after his death, it was his picture which occupied the first page of the Bazaar Handbook.

This fascinating booklet (*Price Sixpence*) laid down some rules for patrons:

> "Change on no account will be forced on Customers against their will. Should anyone feel that they have not spent as much as they might have done, their conscience may find rest in another visit."
>
> "Every person leaving is requested to send two friends in."

The programme of entertainments was lavish: Five concerts, one by St Mary's Choir, and another by the Infant Department of the School; Minstrel Entertainment by St Mary's Minstrels, Glasgow; the Bands of the Rifle and Artillery Volunteers; Organ Recitals; Messrs E. McEleny's and McHenery's String Bands.

Among other special attractions were: The Wonderful Phonograph; Exhibition and Demonstration of Rontgen Rays; Fortune Telling by Madame Clair Voyante; Photography by Maloney Flashlight; "Waccination Gratis" by Professor Herr Von Dummi, the Famous Wax Work Virtuoso.

And a grand Washing Competition:

"Competitors are each supplied with a pail, some cold water, and half-a-bar of Sunlight Soap, also two pegs and a dirty tea cloth. On the word "Go" all wash the cloths. Prize to the competitor who shows the cleanest cloth in the space of three minutes, the same being correctly pegged on the line."

The prizes were donated by Lever Brothers Ltd., "Soapmakers to Her Majesty the Queen": "First Prize, a Handsome Case of Best Quality Electro-Plate Tea Spoons and Tongs, value 15s; Second Prize, Quarter-Gross Case of Sunlight Soap."

The Handbook carried fascinating advertisements for everything from Incandescent Gas Burners to "Snow Boots, Overshoes and Foot Holds". (Why don't we wear such sensible things nowadays?)

Miss O'Brien's china shop in the Vennel advertised a Great Clearance Sale, offering 40-piece tea sets from 9/- (*45p*), and 61-piece dinner sets from 15/- (*75p*).

James Black & Son of Terrace Road was selling Dining Room Suites from £10, and Drawing Room Suites from £12.10s (*£12.50p*).

John McGiveran, Tailor and Clothier of Brymner Street, had suits from 50/- (*£2.50p*) and overcoats from 45/- (*£2.25p*).

The Cathcart Rubber Company in the Square had footballs from 1/- (*5p*) to 10/6 (*52½p*) and boxing gloves from 5/6 (*27½p*) to 15/6 (*77½p*).

A distinguished visitor to the Bazaar was Bishop Hugh Macdonald of Aberdeen, who as a young priest had been a curate in St Mary's for a year.[1]

The Bazaar was a resounding success. Sufficient funds were raised to purchase a disused school in Duncan Street from the Burgh School Board. This now housed the boys of St Mary's. The overall Headmaster was James McLernan. At East Shaw Street the girls were in the charge of Sister Mary Felicitas, and Sister Mary Placida had care of the Infants.

St Mary's Clergy at the turn of the century. Left to right: Rev Charles Edward Fleming, Dean Alexander Taylor, Rev Andrew Lynch and Rev Charles Mann.

1. He left Greenock in 1870 to join the Redemptorists.

CHAPTER FOURTEEN

Into a New Century

THE Twentieth Century opened with the country engaged in war with the Boers in South Africa. Queen Victoria died after a reign of 63 years. The population of Greenock now stood at just over 68,000, nearly a quarter of whom were Catholics.

As the country mourned the Queen, there was more sadness at St Mary's with the early and unexpected death of one of the curates, thirty-seven year old Father Charles Mann. After several years' service in his native Aberdeenshire he had volunteered for Glasgow Archdiocese, and been sent to Greenock in 1897, "endearing himself by his engaging character to priests and people alike."[1] He was a quiet man, of reserved character, "richly endowed intellectually."[1] He is buried in Greenock Cemetery.

Soon afterwards there was happier news as Father Taylor was installed as a Canon of St Andrew's Cathedral, Glasgow. "He received numerous tokens of the esteem of the people, the League of the Cross presenting him with a set of robes, the congregation with a purse of one hundred sovereigns, and his Protestant admirers . . . with a like sum."[2]

Towards the end of the year (1901) he was a guest at the opening of the splendid new St Lawrence's Church in Carnock Street.

Canon Taylor's last major project was to build an extension to the Rectory, which was now rather cramped, with four priests plus

1. *Catholic Directory*, 1902.
2. *Catholicity in Greenock.*

domestic staff, and accommodation needed for visiting clergy. The extension, completed in 1902, can be seen from Houston Street. It cost around £1000. The same year saw the death of the great Archbishop Eyre. He was succeeded by his Vicar General, Canon John Maguire.

* * *

A virulent and prolonged outbreak of smallpox hit the town. The two young curates, Frs Gibbons and O'Leary, had come on loan from Ireland immediately after Ordination, as so many Irish priests did. It was noted how attentive they were to those stricken by the dreadful disease. "Father O'Leary risked his life daily and day and night alike found him at the post of duty."[1]

Fr Gibbons contracted smallpox, "and for a time his life was depaired of. . . Deep and fervent were the prayers for his recovery. It pleased the Almighty to spare him and so delighted were the people of the congregation and so grateful for the noble work accomplished that they presented him with a very substantial testimonial at a great meeting in the Town Hall.[2]

* * *

In the winter of 1904-5 a young priest friend of Canon Taylor's was staying at St Mary's. This was Fr Alexander Macdonald who had been brought up in Greenock after moving from Lochaber with his parents when he was very young. As a little boy at St Mary's school

V. Rev. Alexander Canon Taylor officiating at the launch of a yacht in Messrs. Scott & Co.'s Dock, Greenock.

1. *Glasgow Observer*, 11 November 1905.
2. Ibid, 27 May 1911.

"his early piety and intelligence attracted the attention of . . . Canon Taylor who sent him to Blairs in the summer of 1885."[1] He was ordained after further studies at Valladolid, one of many vocations to the priesthood from St Mary's over the years.

Unfortunately his health deteriorated to the point where he could no longer cope with parish work. "It was suggested to him to take up work in a more suitable climate, but he was unwilling to leave his native land and he replied that his only ambition was to die in harness in his own diocese."[1]

He was allowed to spend the winter of 1903 in Spain, but in the following months his health broke down completely, and he was forced to leave his post in St Patrick's, Anderston, and return to his home parish.

The whole town was stunned when the seemingly robust Canon Taylor died first.

For about a fortnight he had been feeling slightly unwell, but carried on as usual, and on Friday 6 January 1905 he celebrated the nine o'clock Mass for the feast of the Epiphany. Just before lunch time he suddenly collapsed with a massive heart attack. Fr Macdonald was with him, and administered Extreme Unction.

The newspaper reports convey the sense of shock and great loss felt by the whole town.

As was to be expected, his funeral was a huge affair, with a packed church, crowds gathered in the street outside, and police on hand to direct the traffic.

In the sanctuary hung with black and white draperies, Archbishop Maguire presided at the solemn Requiem at which the late Canon's two cousins were celebrant and deacon. The music was provided by a choir of fifteen priests directed by Rev. Dr Rogan, a former curate of St Mary's. The preacher was Fr William O'Brien, another former curate.

At the end of Mass the coffin was lowered into the vault where the remains of Dean Gordon rested

Canon Taylor was aged 61 at his death, and had served St Mary's for a record thirty-seven years.

Just under four months later young Father Macdonald also died. He was only 37. His funeral took place at St Patrick's, Anderston.

* * *

1. *Catholic Directory*, 1906.

THEN . . . AND NOW

Photograph by Gerard Ralston

One of the many priests who attended Canon Taylor's funeral was Rev. Patrick Houlihan of Lambhill in Glasgow, who within the month was appointed to take charge of St Mary's. Any change of Parish Priest is naturally the subject of much anxious speculation, and this was all the more intense now since Canon Taylor had been at the helm for such a long time. Many mature parishioners had spent their entire lives under his regime.

The news of the new appointment was greeted with considerable relief. Fr Houlihan had "a splendid record of zealous service to the Church, and . . . a reputation of being a sterling Irishman and a kindly and courteous gentleman."[1]

However, the people of his old parish were heartbroken, and Fr Houlihan himself was reportedly none too pleased. He was very happy in Lambhill, where he had finally begun to enjoy the fruits of eighteen years' labour, having just completed a massive building programme: "a noble church, excellent schools, recreation rooms . . . and a commodious presbytery."[1] (The "noble church" of St Agnes, which at the time seemed far too large for its congregation, was known locally as "Houlihan's Folly"!) And now he had to leave it all behind.

The story goes that one morning soon after his arrival in Greenock he was on a visit to East Shaw Street school, where after speaking to the children he spent some time chatting to the teacher. Naturally the little ears in the front row were wide open, and he was heard to say how unhappy he was at having to move to Greenock. As the dinner time bell rang he set off for home. Halfway up Walker's Brae (West Stewart Street) a small girl skipped past. She stopped and turned back. Gazing sadly up at him with big blue eyes she asked, "Do you not like us, Father?" Struck with remorse, he there and then resolved to stop complaining and make the best of the situation. And indeed, he served St Mary's well for the next seventeen years.

1. *The Catholic Herald*, 28 June 1907.

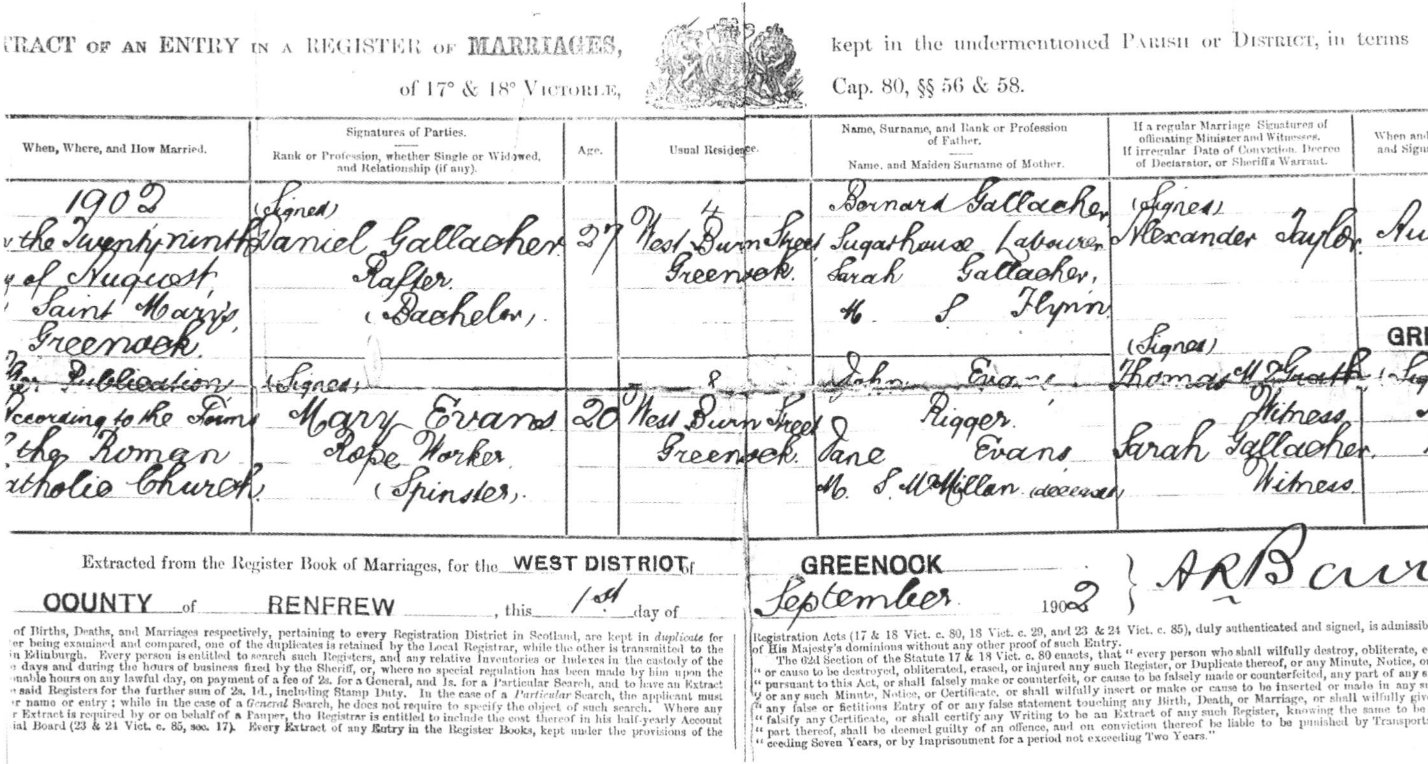

[EXT]RACT OF AN ENTRY IN A REGISTER OF MARRIAGES, kept in the undermentioned PARISH or DISTRICT, in terms of 17° & 18° VICTORIÆ, Cap. 80, §§ 56 & 58.

When, Where, and How Married.	Signatures of Parties. Rank or Profession, whether Single or Widowed, and Relationship (if any).	Age.	Usual Residence.	Name, Surname, and Rank or Profession of Father. Name, and Maiden Surname of Mother.	If a regular Marriage Signatures of officiating Minister and Witnesses. If irregular Date of Conviction, Decree of Declarator, or Sheriff's Warrant.	When and ... and Signat[ure]
1902 ... the Twenty-ninth ... of August ... Saint Mary's, Greenock. ... Publication ... According to the Form ... the Roman ... Catholic Church.	(Signed) Daniel Gallacher Rafter (Bachelor).	27	4 West Burn Street Greenock.	Bernard Gallacher Sugarhouse Labourer Sarah Gallacher, M. S. Flynn	(Signed) Alexander Taylor.	Aug ...
	(Signed) Mary Evans Rope Worker (Spinster).	20	8 West Burn Street Greenock.	John Evans Rigger. Jane Evans M. S. McMillan (deceased)	(Signed) Thomas McGrath Witness. Sarah Gallacher. Witness.	

Extracted from the Register Book of Marriages, for the WEST DISTRICT of GREENOCK
COUNTY of RENFREW, this 1st day of September 1902 } A R Bain

... of Births, Deaths, and Marriages respectively, pertaining to every Registration District in Scotland, are kept in *duplicate* for ... being examined and compared, one of the duplicates is retained by the Local Registrar, while the other is transmitted to the ... in Edinburgh. Every person is entitled to search such Registers, and any relative Inventories or Indexes in the custody of the ... days and during the hours of business fixed by the Sheriff, or, where no special regulation has been made by him upon the ... able hours on any lawful day, on payment of a fee of 2s. for a General, and 1s. for a Particular Search, and to have an Extract ... said Registers for the further sum of 2s. 1d., including Stamp Duty. In the case of a *Particular* Search, the applicant must ... name or entry; while in the case of a *General* Search, he does not require to specify the object of such search. Where any ... Extract is required by or on behalf of a Pauper, the Registrar is entitled to include the cost thereof in his half-yearly Account ... ial Board (23 & 24 Vict. c. 85, sec. 17). Every Extract of any Entry in the Register Books, kept under the provisions of the Registration Acts (17 & 18 Vict. c. 80, 18 Vict. c. 29, and 23 & 24 Vict. c. 85), duly authenticated and signed, is admissible ... of His Majesty's dominions without any other proof of such Entry.

The 62d Section of the Statute 17 & 18 Vict. c. 80 enacts, that "every person who shall wilfully destroy, obliterate, era[se] ... or cause to be destroyed, obliterated, erased, or injured any such Register, or Duplicate thereof, or any Minute, Notice, or ... pursuant to this Act, or shall falsely make or counterfeit, or cause to be falsely made or counterfeited, any part of any such ... or any such Minute, Notice, or Certificate, or shall wilfully insert or make or cause to be inserted or made in any such ... any false or fictitious Entry of or any false statement touching any Birth, Death, or Marriage, or shall wilfully give ... falsify any Certificate, or shall certify any Writing to be an Extract of any such Register, knowing the same to be fa[lse] ... part thereof, shall be deemed guilty of an offence, and on conviction thereof be liable to be punished by Transportati[on] ... ceeding Seven Years, or by Imprisonment for a period not exceeding Two Years."

A marriage certificate of 1902, showing typical occupations: a sugarhouse labourer, a rafter (working at the Port Glasgow timber ponds), a rope worker, a rigger (dock-worker).

CHAPTER FIFTEEN

Rev. Patrick Houlihan "A Sterling Irishman"

FATHER Houlihan was a hustler. An assessment in the wonderfully flowery oratory of the period: "Some thought our new priest was framed in too gentle a mould for the bustle and turmoil of a busy centre . . . How little they knew that under that quiet, gentle and unostentatious exterior there beat a heart, gentle 'tis true, but brave, restless, resolute, and undaunted where lay God's work."[1] (We don't make sentences like that any more!)

Rev. Patrick Houlihan

A moderniser, he soon had the telephone installed in the Rectory — the phone number was 22Y! He also purchased the ground adjoining the church to the west, when the opportunity arose.

Just a few months after his arrival disaster struck. Imagine the consternation of the people arriving for Mass one Sunday morning in August 1905, as the

1. James J. Cook, quoted in *The Catholic Herald*, 28 June 1907.

news spread: "Have you heard? There was a fire at the Girls' School last night!" And indeed, the top flat of the East Shaw Street school was gutted. This was a blow, for finances as usual were stretched to the limit.

Temporary accommodation was found for the pupils in the Sir Michael Street Hall, and Fr Houlihan set about organising the reconstruction of the school. He took the opportunity to add an extra storey to the building, thus turning disaster to good account.

* * *

Like his predecessors, Fr Houlihan took an intense interest in education. His greatest achievement was the establishment of St Mary's Higher Grade School. More and more Catholic parents were anxious for their children to receive Secondary education. In Greenock they attended Holmscroft Higher Grade School (later called the Mount School), or, if their parents could afford to send them, boys could go to St Mungo's or St Aloysius' in Glasgow, and girls to St Margaret's Convent, Paisley.

Fr Houlihan's great dream was to establish a Catholic Secondary School in the area, and this was achieved in a remarkably short time by phenomenal efforts from the whole Catholic community in the Three Burghs of Greenock, Gourock and Port Glasgow.

In 1907 Fr Houlihan purchased two villas with adjoining land at a cost of over £3,000. The site was conveniently close to the church at the corner of Patrick Street and Houston Street. It was asserted at the time that "from the openness of its situation (it) may claim to be one of the healthiest locations in Greenock"![1]

The cost of the new building was to be around £10,000, and every stone had to be paid for by the people themselves. Intense fundraising took place in the four parishes of St Mary's, St Lawrence's, St John's and St Ninian's: "Grand Balls", whist drives, raffles, sales of work, evening cruises, jumble sales, "miles of pennies" . . .

At this time, too, the church was closed for four months while major repairs were carried out to the roof, after which redecoration was necessary. Archbishop Maguire officiated at the re-opening on 29 September 1907.

* * *

1. *Bazaar Handbook*, 1912.

Meanwhile a happy Parish celebration took place to mark Fr Houlihan's Silver Jubilee. Despite his protests, for he was a quiet, self-effacing man, it was a splendid affair. (All the same, one wonders why it took a committee of fifty-nine gentlemen to organise it!)

A "large and enthusiastic gathering filled every part of the Town Hall"[1] for a concert, mainly of Irish songs, during which a presentation was made of the usual one hundred sovereigns. One of the speakers, Bishop MacFarlane of Dunkeld raised a laugh by remarking on the inappropriateness of presenting gold sovereigns to celebrate a Silver Jubilee. However, the recipient made no objection!

The fulsome tributes which were paid to Fr Houlihan showed how completely he had gained the admiration and affection of his people in a very short time.

The evening closed with the singing of "Faith of our Fathers".

Interestingly, Bishop MacFarlane remarked that as a very young man nearly forty years before, he used to come down on visits to "the late Dean Gordon, a very dear friend of his youth. (Applause.)[1]

The Bishop seemed to enjoy his visits to Greenock, which, he said, had "a climate that was celebrated for being very briny, very bracing, and very salubrious, and . . . an atmosphere that was sweetened by the fumes of the Glebe Sugar House. (Laughter.)"[1]

He observed that "the acquaintance he had made at that time with the congregation and with the spirit of the congregation was such that he always looked back with pleasure to the days passed down there."[1]

Among the gifts from the schoolchildren, Fr Houlihan received an embroidered silk cushion for use in church, a tortoise-shell handled umbrella, and "a magnificent tea-cosy".[1]

The following year Fr Houlihan was made a Canon of the Cathedral Chapter. And early in 1909 his dream began to be realised, as with great delight he cut the first sod on the site of the new school.. "The contractors . . . presented the Canon with a handsome silver wheelbarrow".[2]

One of the villas on the site had been demolished to make way for the new school. In the other, which occupied the site of the present playground, the Higher Grade Department was established, under the Headship of William Horgan B.A., an Irish graduate, as were most of the teaching staff. This was the first Catholic Higher Grade School in the West of Scotland outside Glasgow. Meanwhile work on the new

1. *Catholic Herald*, 28 June, 1907.
2. *Catholicity in Greenock*, p28.

building proceeded rapidly. The classes in the villa must have had a trying year with the noise and distracting activity round about them.

On his way home after serving early morning Mass, eight-year-old Harry Kilpatrick used to dawdle in Patrick Street, watching his uncle who was one of the stone-masons "in their long open-sided sheds cutting by hand the red sandstone blocks that were slowly rising to form the massive structure that was to be our future palatial school."[1] Harry's grandfather, who arrived from Antrim around 1850, had also been a stone-mason, and had worked on the construction of St Mary's church. The little boy who watched with such interest the building of the school never dreamed that one day he would be its headmaster.

* * *

In 1909 there was published (*Price Twopence*) the interesting little booklet "*Catholicity in Greenock*". Subtitled "*A Story of a Century's Wonderful Progress*", it marked the centenary of the opening of the Greenock Mission by Rev. John Davidson,

A manifestation of popular piety at the time was membership of the various parish societies. Those of St Mary's are listed by the pamphlet's anonymous author: "Mount Carmel, Living Rosary, St

Canon Houlihan with St Mary's first Higher Grade pupils, outside the villa which served as their temporary school. ***Photo: Greenock Telegraph.***

1. Henry J. Kilpatrick, *Notre Dame School Magazine*, 1993.

Vincent de Paul, League of the Cross (with juvenile branch), Young Men's Society, Altar Society, Children of Mary, Sacred Heart (for men and women), and Holy Angels (for girls). Under the kindly and energetic supervision of Canon Houlihan, all are flourishing, and the position of St Mary's is most satisfactory and encouraging."

* * *

The boys of St Mary's at this time were split between the school in Duncan Street and the "dark and dingy hovel" in Sir Michael Street (where one of the teachers was future headmaster Joe McCurdy, who gave such long and outstanding service to education in Greenock. Over fifty years later he was still teaching, having been called out of retirement to take the Preparatory class in St Columba's, at a time of teacher shortage.)

Many years later Harry Kilpatrick still had vivid memories of the great day in 1910 when the new school was completed: "I can still recall the thrill it was to march from Duncan Street down to Patrick Street and take possession of the new roomy, lofty, airy, comfortable, well-furnished classrooms — for so they seemed to us. The Higher Grade Department . . . took over the top flat, with its Science Room and Art Room, unequalled in those days, on the bottom flat, off the Assembly Hall . . .There was a Woodwork room and a Cookery room, also extremely well-equipped." The Janitor "a Sergeant Peacock, who was also our drill master," was housed on the ground floor with his wife and family. "The Headmaster in those days occupied the highest room in the school — well away from trouble!"[1]

Among certain sections of the town prejudice lingered. It is recounted that in the beginning the younger children had to be escorted to and from school by fathers and older relatives to protect them from stone-throwers.

It must be said that bigotry was not, of course, one-sided! An old story concerns the League of the Cross, a temperance society, which flourished in St Mary's during the late nineteenth and early twentieth centuries. In its heyday the League formed a band, and managed to purchase second-hand Hussars' uniforms, very splendid, blue with gold facings on the tunic and a yellow stripe on the trousers. On the day of their first parade they set off proudly marching to the church along the Vennel in the town centre. Out of a close rushed a man with

1. Henry J. Kilpatrick, op cit.

a pot of boiling tripe snatched off the fire. He hurled it through the big drum, yelling: "Away, ye Orange b______s!"

* * *

At first the Higher Grade went up to Third Year only, when pupils could sit for the Intermediate Certificate before continuing their Secondary education elsewhere. "Pupils who intended to leave

St Mary's Higher Grade School, opened in 1910. ***Photograph: Rev. James McGhee***

A "physical culture" lesson in the "Grand Hall" of the new Higher Grade School.
Photo: Greenock Telegraph

when they were fourteen . . . went into the 'Supplementary' classes."[1]

The teachers were a heroic band, with a true sense of vocation. "Few of them", recalls Harry Kilpatrick, "were paid as much as £1 a week!" They were appointed and paid by the Parish Priest, who had the constant worry of trying to make ends meet, and could only afford to pay them a pittance. The responsibility for the Higher Grade was, of course, shared by the four local parishes, and all struggled under the crushing financial burden of supporting their schools, "as well as contributing to the non-denominational schools through rates and taxes".[2]

Canon Houlihan made his regular rounds of the Parish collecting for the school, accompanied by a stalwart parishioner who carried the money bag. It was well known that when visiting the house of a needy family the Canon would take out of the bag instead of putting in. So he often enough could not afford to pay salaries in full, from the piles of pennies and threepenny bits he kept on his mantlepiece, and many were the tales of poverty among teachers.

Typical was the young lady who wore her one white blouse day after day, carefully washed and ironed each night, while the lace collar and cuffs became more and more frayed. It was her only blouse and she couldn't afford another.

Dan Kelly, another future headmaster, took a second job to support his growing family. He worked at the docks late into the night tallying ships' cargoes. He was mortified when one day, exhausted, he fell asleep at his desk. Thereafter his young daughter Sheila, who was a pupil in his class, had instructions to leave her seat and quietly waken her father if she saw him nodding off again.

(Dan Kelly established something of a teaching dynasty in Greenock, as his four daughters and his granddaughter later taught in the town.)

In 1912 the total number on the rolls of St Mary's Schools (Patrick Street and East Shaw Street) was 1,903, the average daily attendance being 1,686.

To help pay off the building costs of the school, parishioners once again organised a three-day Bazaar in the Town Hall in October 1912. Admission for half a day cost 6d, rising to 1/- (*5p*) on Saturday afternoon. Attractions this time included a Gipsy Tent, Electric Fish Pond, Lub in a Tub (What?), and Hoop-la, as well as concerts, organ

1. Henry J. Kilpatrick, op cit.
2. Thomas P. F. Murray, *St Columba's High School Golden Jubilee* booklet.

recitals, and "A Superb Exhibition of the Famous BB Pictures". The Bazaar was a great success, and reached its target figure of £2,000.

* * *

In 1914 Canon Houlihan invited the Marist Brothers to take charge of the Higher Grade Department, and Brother Lewis became Headmaster with a salary of £220 a year. Assistant teachers were to receive £100. The annual salary of a teacher in the Elementary Division was £90.

In the previous year the Franciscan Sisters had moved from Bank Street to "Glenlea" in Madeira Street, where they continued to run their private school.

* * *

Despite poor health, Canon Houlihan continued to work at a furious rate, undertaking further extensive improvements to the church building in 1914, including the installation of electric light, doing away with the "elegant gas fittings".

St Mary's "All-Ireland Team", 1912. Back, left to right: Rev William Ryan, Rev Thomas Wall. Front, left to right: Rev Michael O'Donoghue, Canon Houlihan, Rev Michael Fitzpatrick.

The sacristy was partly demolished and rebuilt to form a Lady Chapel. A new sacristy was built, with a vestment case of fine Austrian oak, to be constructed "in such a way as to be absolutely dust-proof".[1]

A new baptistery was built. Unfortunately this necessitated the removal of the "most exquisite spiral staircase in wood-work"[2] which led to the choir gallery. The new side door adjoining the baptistery was surmounted by a shield whose significance is rather mysterious. It shows the letter "P" and what could be interpreted as an unusual "chi-rho" symbol. "P" may stand for Pius (X), the reigning Pope.

A new stone staircase was put in the tower, where the original baptistery had been. An impressive doorway was made in the tower,

The altar in the new Lady Chapel, 1914.

1. Job specification, St Mary's Archives.
2. *Catholic Directory*,1863.

and a small entrance porch formed, replacing the original vestibule, and allowing space for extra seating. The church was furnished with new benches in Austrian oak.

The organ gallery was extended, a new confessional was installed, the whole church was re-floored, with terrazzo replacing flagstones in the aisles. A small oratory was constructed in the house, with window looking into the church.

The most welcome of Canon Houlihan's innovations was no doubt the "heating apparatus", consisting of pipes running the length of the church along the floor. No wonder he was popular!

The whole was to cost £2,203.15/-

The Canon had a heroic faith that the money would be found somehow. And it was!

A SAINT MARY'S GHOST STORY

Mrs Jean Jeffrey, born in 1913, heard this story from her mother.

ONCE a man, whom we will call Joe, had no place to stay. He hid in the church as it was being locked up for the night.

When all was quiet he went and lay down on a bench near the front, and soon fell asleep.

Suddenly, he woke up, hearing a voice. It was still dark, but the altar candles were lit. The voice repeated: "Is there anyone here who can serve Mass?"

Joe sat up. "I'm here," he said, "but I've never served Mass."

There was a priest at the altar, who gave him a card with the responses, and they proceeded with Mass.

Afterwards the priest explained that he had promised to say Mass for someone, but had forgotten.

"A good thing you remembered, then, Father," said Joe.

"I didn't remember," said the priest, "before I died!"

CHAPTER SIXTEEN

War and After

IN AUGUST 1914 Pope Pius X died, heartbroken, it was said, at the outbreak of the First World War. With his great devotion to the Eucharist, he had brought about changes which affected the spiritual life of ordinary Catholics. At his urging people were slowly beginning to accept the idea of receiving Holy Communion more often than a few times a year. He is probably best remembered for lowering the First Communion age for children to around seven. He also revived the use of Gregorian Chant in the liturgy, and this was becoming more widespread. A small plaque at the Sacred Heart altar commemorates this saintly Pope.

The outbreak of war had an immediate effect on Patrick Street School, which was requisitioned by the War Office to accommodate troops. Pupils were transferred to East Shaw Street, and attended school for only half a day. This continued for a year till the military camp at Wood Street was completed. The children resumed to their normal schooling, while their fathers and older brothers went off to have their lives thrown away in the trenches.

One of St Mary's curates, Rev. William Ryan from Waterford, volunteered for the British army. He served as a chaplain in France for two years and was badly wounded during the Battle of the Somme. "He was asleep in a dug-out with other officers when a shell killed the officers on each side of him and wounded him about the thighs."[1] He was mentioned in despatches for devotion to duty.

1. *Glasgow Observer*, 6 January 1917.

There was plenty of war work for those left behind, for example in the Torpedo Factory and the shipyards, which were busy as never before. There was a fair measure of prosperity and people were making money. But this was a bubble which quickly burst, and hard times were ahead. When the war ended the country was nearly bankrupt.

In his history of the town J. L. Dow sketches some of the effects of war: "Many thousands of Greenockians had served with the colours, and in the merchant navy. Of these 1,500 did not return. The human and social consequences of this appalling waste cannot be calculated, but at the same time cannot be over-stressed. Families were left without their breadwinner; children grew up without the influence of their father. A new generation of children remained unborn.

"Another consequence of war is the interruption to the careers of the young, called to serve their country at the age of eighteen and coming back grown men, without the training in trade and profession to equip them for the long years to come. There is, too, the fact of war's over-emphasis on the manufactures necessary for the prosecution of war, and the consequent neglect of others needed for the demands of peace. Housebuilding, for example, had practically stopped for five years, and with the complete disruption of international trade during those years, industries depending on the import and export of goods not essential to war, consequently declined."[1] The process of recovery was hard and slow.

* * *

After the war, far-reaching changes in education took place in 1918 with the passing of the Education (Scotland) Act, which took the Catholic schools into the state system. Now "Catholic schools would be maintained by public money for the first time, thereby freeing the Catholics from the double penalty of paying for the state schools out of rates and taxes and then having to fund their own schools."[2]

The Act gave an absolute guarantee that the religious character of Catholic schools would be safeguarded for the future.

Catholic teachers now received a massive pay rise (sometimes as much as a hundred per cent) as their salaries were brought into line with those of their colleagues in the state schools. As Tom Murray remarks: "Previously, as well as possessing a vocation, Catholic teachers were forced to accept a vow of poverty."[2]

1. J. L. Dow, *Greenock*, p102.
2. Thomas P. F. Murray, *St Columba's High School Golden Jubilee* booklet, p9.

Canon Houlihan was elected to the Education Authority which replaced the old Burgh School Board.

The story of St Mary's Schools has been rather like that of the Magic Porridge Pot, which kept overflowing. Yet again more accommodation was needed, and one of the Canon's last acts was to purchase and transfer to the local Education Authority a former Approved School in Captain Street, to house the girls from East Shaw Street.

* * *

The human dynamo that was Patrick Houlihan was now at last running out of energy. Never physically robust, it was astounding what he achieved since his reluctant arrival at St Mary's. "Hard work had undermined what little strength he had, and as the result of a chill . . . he became seriously ill. He was removed to a nursing home in Glasgow, but made little progress towards recovery. He was brought back to Greenock and seemed at times to be regaining strength, but in reality the end was near. He gradually became weaker, and on the evening of Thursday, the 4th January (1923), he passed peacefully away. The funeral took place on the following Monday, when the mortal remains were laid to rest in the vault of St Mary's Church."[1]

Rev. John McMillan

His replacement was the Rev. John McMillan, born in Glasgow and ordained in Rome in 1898.

* * *

A snapshot of the Parish in 1924 shows that by now there were no fewer than six priests at St Mary's. The curates were Frs John Walls, John Scanlon, James Ronan, Daniel J. Horgan, and Michael Costello. There were six Sunday Masses, and four on Holidays of Obligation. Parish societies were the Eucharistic League, St Vincent de Paul,

1. *Catholic Directory*, 1924.

Rev John McMillan with the Choir, shortly after his arrival in 1923. In the middle of the back row, sixth from the right, is John Gillespie, whose great-grandson, Fr John Tormey, became Parish Priest of St Mary's in 2000.

Photograph by Jessie Hamilton

League of the Cross, Children of Mary, Sacred Heart Confraternity, Angels' Guild (for girls), Boys' Guild, Propagation of the Faith.

The church Choir was renowned throughout the district. Bishop Hay would have been amazed! The new Parish Priest had a great interest in Church Music. Soon after his arrival he sat with the Choir for a group photograph where they can be seen in all their finery, the ladies in their wonderful 1920s hats. I with we could hear them!

The boys' school in Patrick Street had an average daily attendance of 910. The girls' school in Captain Street averaged 878, and the infants in East Shaw Street 645. The two latter were combined under one Head, the gentle Sister Genevieve, with Sister Theresa as Infants' Mistress.

Fr McMillan was later to write that "his greatest delight was to be surrounded by the infants and small children from St Mary's School on the Town Hall platform on St Patrick's night when their annual concerts were a feature of the whole town."[1]

The Higher Grade school had a roll of 320, having become a full six-year school in 1922.

The Choir in 2001. Not so elegant as their predecessors, but just as keen! *Back row:* l. to r. Bill Fitzharris, Steve Cullen, Tom Glancy, John Kennedy, Jim McGonigal. *Middle row:* Michelle Liddell, Helen Kirkwood, Katrina McLellan, Mary Kennedy, Mary Teresa Burrows, Felicity Bryant, Ann Williams. *Front row:* Mary Gallacher, Catherine Phillips, Margaret Garvie, Julie Hall, Marion O'Donnell, Gregory McHugh (Musical Director). *Missing: Elena Dusi, Elizabeth Lavelle, Dan McCormick, Eddie McGeehan, Sadie McGonigal.*

1. *St Patrick's School Centenary Booklet*, p24.

With numbers continuing to grow, the time had come to form a new parish in Greenock, and in 1924 St Mary's was subdivided to form St Patrick's, with the former school in Duncan Street being given over to serve as a temporary church. Its first priest was Rev. James P. Kelly D.D.

* * *

1924 was an important year for the Franciscan Sisters. In January they celebrated the Golden Jubilee of their arrival in Greenock, and in September they joined in celebrations to mark the coming of Franciscans to Britain in 1224. (They reached Scotland in 1231.)

For the January Jubilee Fr McMillan celebrated Mass in the Convent Chapel, Madeira Street. Sister Fidelis was present, the only surviving member of the little band of five pioneers who arrived in 1874.

As well as teaching, the Sisters were involved in running the Parish societies. They also visited the Prison and the sick.

* * *

On 7 December the church was filled for the dedication of the beautiful new Lady Altar, to which parishioners had subscribed as a memorial to Canon Houlihan.

It is reported that while money was being collected rumours began to fly around. How could the new Parish Priest afford to buy a

The new Lady Altar, erected in 1927 as a memorial to Canon Houlihan.

car, an unheard-of luxury for a priest in those days? Was it possible that some of the fund had been diverted? Poor Fr McMillan eventually found it necessary to deny the rumours from the pulpit, and reveal that his little Ford had been a generous gift from his former parishioners in St Anthony's, Govan. A salutary lesson against jumping to conclusions!

In 1927 Sister Genevieve died, to be succeeded by the redoubtable Sister Theresa, who remained until her retiral in 1950, having notched up thirty-four years' service to St Mary's Girls' School, twenty-three of them as Headmistress.

Life was hard in these years of Depression and the Hungry Thirties. Industry was in decline and unemployment soared. A survey in 1930 showed that compared to the national unemployment rate of "12.6% of all insured workers", in Greenock the rate was 33.3%. Conditions were grim, with soup kitchens having to be set up for a time. The same survey showed that for families living in the central area the average weekly income was £1.17s (*£1.85p*), while in other parts of the town family income ranged from 10/- (*50p*) to £11.6s.10d per week. (A teacher earned around £11 a month.) Average rents were 4/- (*20p*) a week for a "single end", and 6/1 (*30p*) for three

A back land tenement behind Market Street, before slum clearances in the 1930s.
Photograph: Watt Library

apartments. This was a time of great hardship, for the many who were living in extreme poverty, particularly in the overcrowded, disease-ridden central area, where in 1933 more than 2,000 houses were declared unfit for human habitation.

However, things began to look a little brighter with an upturn in shipbuilding, and the improvements in living conditions which were now taking place. The water supply was upgraded; sewage was processed in a new modern plant instead of being discharged straight into the East India Harbour; slum clearances began around Market Street, the Vennel, and Dalrymple Street. The old tenements were demolished and the people decanted to new houses in outlying districts like Belville Street, Bow Farm and Hole Farm. Old lanes with evocative names disappeared: Mince Collop Close, Jib Boom Close, Jacob's Ladder. The Vennel was replaced by the new High Street (swept away in its turn by still later improvements).

From this point the population of St Mary's fell steadily as churches were built in the outlying districts to serve new housing schemes: St Mungo's (1934), St Joseph's (1947), St Andrew's (1951).

The slum clearances had an immediate effect on the town's appalling health picture. The death rate for 1933 was the lowest on record, and infant mortality had begun to decline.

* * *

The Legion of Mary was established in the Parish with the help of

The Legion of Mary, 2001. *Standing:* l. to r. Christine Moran, Kathleen O'Rourke, Margaret Lafferty. *Seated:* Marion O'Donnell, Eileen Feen.

Legionaries from Glasgow, and seven members were enrolled at the first meeting on 2 December 1932.

Extracts from a report to the Legion Curia in May 1933 give an idea of the varied work they engaged in:

"The Legionaries have full charge of five of the Guilds of the Sacred Heart Confraternity and visit the members monthly. . . Four of the Legionaries assist with the work of the Girls' Club which . . . is conducted by the Catholic Women's League . . . Two Legionaries are members of the C.W.L. Foreign Mission Sewing Guild . . . The Legionaries have been given the names of many of the sick of the Parish and these are visited in their homes each week. The Legionaries also have permission to visit the Hospital for Consumptives attached to Smithston Poorhouse; they go there twice a week on Thursdays and Sundays for an hour and give instructions to 3 children there. The Borstal for Girls attached to the Prison at Gateside is also visited by Legionaries on Sundays . . . From last week the work of our Praesidium will be house to house visitation, with distribution of Catholic Papers."

* * *

As usual, the schools were overcrowded. A new Secondary School was planned on what the *Greenock Telegraph* called "an ideal site" away up in the country, at Peat Road. St Columba's was opened on 16 June 1933 by Archbishop Donald Mackintosh of Glasgow. Brother Bonaventure moved from Patrick Street to become the first Rector. Joe McCurdy was the new Headmaster of Patrick Street School, comprising Elementary boys' classes, and what were now known as Junior Secondary boys.

Excess numbers were taught in what became known as "Tosh's Academy" — premises in Houston Street formerly occupied by Tosh the Builder, less than ideal accommodation for school classes! Later, huts were built to house the Technical Department.

Junior Secondary girls moved into the former "Buroo School" in Dalrymple Street, so called "having been built at the request of the local Employment Bureau for the training of the many unemployed young people of those days".[1] It was now dedicated to Our Lady of Loreto.

In Captain Street the overcrowding was eased with the removal of

1. H. J. Kilpatrick, *Notre Dame School Magazine*, 1993.

Advanced Division pupils. In 1936 H.M Inspector was pleased that "no class had a roll exceeding fifty pupils"!

* * *

A great benefactor of the church around this time was Miss Mary Devlin, who had a fruiterer's business in Grey Place. She donated a beautiful marble pulpit and altar rails. Unfortunately, the pulpit was never seen to advantage as one side was almost up against a pillar. It was decorated with reliefs: on the front panel the Assumption (recalling the church's title), on the sides the Ascension of Our Lord, and the Descent of the Holy Spirit. Statues of the four evangelists adorned the corners. It was much admired, and many parishioners were dismayed that it was dismantled when the remodelling of the Sanctuary was completed in the 1970s.

* * *

The social life of the Parish flourished in these years, with dances and concerts in the Parish hall — the well-remembered Salon in Nelson Street, which Fr McMillan purchased in 1925 at a cost of £2,250. Older parishioners still speak fondly of the Salon, and still regret that it was sold off in the Sixties.

There was a dramatic society under the direction of Fr McGurk. (One of a family of fifteen brothers and sisters from Co. Derry, Fr Aloysius McGurk was well-known as a bit of a dandy — sporting gold cuff-links, a gold-topped walking stick, and . . . spats!)

A thriving tennis club was set up by a group of enterprising young parishioners. They used the tennis court in the extensive grounds of Belltrees, the house at 13 Newark Street adjoining the Franciscan Convent.

Belltrees, acquired by the Sisters around 1930, provided accommodation for Lady Boarders, particularly some of the teachers who had come from Ireland to help staff our schools. Later, the Convent School occupied the ground floor.

Dances and tennis club there may have been, but probably the chief matchmaking agency in the Parish was the Choir! Many a romance sprang up to the strains of *Missa De Angelis*.

CHAPTER SEVENTEEN

The Second World War

AS THE country geared up once again for war, trade and industry improved. Production was stepped up in the shipyards, engine works and Torpedo Factory. By the beginning of 1938 Greenock Chamber of Commerce was able to claim that there were no skilled workers idle — although unemployment continued high among the unskilled.

War preparations intensified. In summer 1939 conscription was introduced. Gas masks were issued, and instructions given for blackout.

On Sunday 3 September war was declared, and immediately Greenock got a taste of what it would mean when survivors of the liner *Athenia* were landed at the Albert Harbour. On her way to Canada with a complement that included many children, she was torpedoed on the very first day of the war.

"The town now got down seriously to defence and security. Baffle walls were built across the mouths of closes, air raid shelters were prepared . . . An emergency relief organisation was set up to deal with evacuation, billeting and feeding homeless families . . . Canteens were opened in various places and were staffed by willing voluntary workers for the servicemen who were in the harbours, and the town, or passing through."[1]

Civil Defence centres were set up. Ration cards were issued, and people were instructed to register with their chosen shopkeeper in

1. J. L. Dow, *Greenock*, p160.

preparation for rationing, which was introduced the following January.

From 1939 to 1941 pupils attended school for half the day only, to safeguard them in case of air-raid. Air-raid drill became a familiar part of the routine.

* * *

Tuesday 30 April 1940, 2.30 p.m. The French destroyer Maille Brezé was lying at the Tail of the Bank. Suddenly an explosion ripped through the ship, as one of her own torpedoes was accidentally discharged. The blast was heard all over town. As far away as Peat Road windows in St Columba's School were shattered. A rescue operation was immediately mounted to try to control the fire and take off survivors before the ship went down. There was confusion and screaming amid fire and smoke. Witnesses later spoke of seeing pressed against the portholes the faces of those who were trapped.

Twenty-eight men died that afternoon, and over sixty were injured. The townsfolk rallied round to help the survivors in any way they could. Some were billeted with local families until the call went out to join De Gaulle's Free French forces.

Marcel Gouis, a young "pompon rouge" from Le Havre, was one

Funeral of the French sailors killed on the Maille Brezé. ***Photograph: Greenock Telegraph***

of those who stayed with the Donnelly family. In a letter dated 10 January 1945 he wrote: "Je n' ai aucune photographie de personne - mais je revois quand même tous mes amis d' Ecosse. Combien de fois ai-je parlé de votre belle Patrie. Tous les Français ayant séjourné en Ecosse sont unanimes à reconnaître l' amabilité et la grande hospitalité des Ecossais."[1]

(I haven't a photograph of anyone, but nevertheless I can still picture all my Scottish friends. I have often spoken of your beautiful country. All the French who spent time in Scotland are unanimous in recognising the kindness and great hospitality of the Scots.)

Requiem Mass for those who died was celebrated in St Mary's, which was packed for the occasion. A large French naval escort accompanied the cortege to the cemetery.

* * *

On 10 June 1940 Italy declared war. and immediately all Italian-born men living in Britain were rounded up to be interned, "even though," as J.L. Dow says, "there were few more law-abiding citizens than

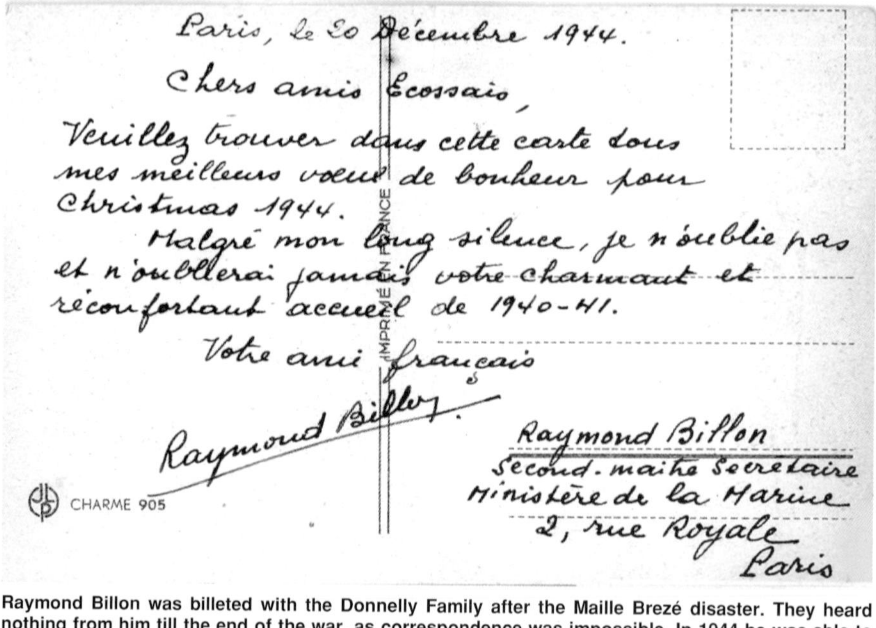

Paris, le 20 Décembre 1944.

Chers amis Ecossais,

Veuillez trouver dans cette carte tous mes meilleurs voeux de bonheur pour Christmas 1944.

Malgré mon long silence, je n'oublie pas et n'oublierai jamais votre charmant et réconfortant accueil de 1940-41.

Votre ami français

Raymond Billon.

Raymond Billon
Second-maître Secrétaire
Ministère de la Marine
2, rue Royale
Paris

CHARME 905

IMPRIMÉ EN FRANCE

Raymond Billon was billeted with the Donnelly Family after the Maille Brezé disaster. They heard nothing from him till the end of the war, as correspondence was impossible. In 1944 he was able to send a Christmas card in which he expresses the feelings of all the "pompons rouges" for their Scottish hosts: *"Despite my long silence, I have not forgotten, and never will forget, your charming and consoling welcome in 1940-41."*

1. Letter in possession of the author.

Greenock's Italian colony. The police were busy bringing them in when bands of young hooligans . . . attacked every Italian shop in the town . . . It was a disgraceful business, though similar lootings took place in most towns."[1]

* * *

In another letter to the Donnellys Marcel wrote: "En 1940 je voyais les bombardiers boches partir pour la Grande Bretagne et je faisais des voeux pour que les bombes vous épargnent."[2]

(In 1940 I used to see the German bombers heading for Great Britain and I prayed that the bombs would spare you.)

In March 1941 Greenockians watched in horror as the sky was lit up by the Clydebank Blitz. It was only a matter of time till it was Greenock's turn.

During air raid alerts most tenement-dwellers sheltered in the ground floor or basement of the steel-reinforced closes. The priests of St Mary's sheltered in the cellar under the house.

Just after midnight on 6 May the sirens sounded. For two hours the town was bombed indiscriminately. In St Mary's Parish the large tenement property at the corner of Robertson Street and South Street was destroyed by a land mine, killing many of those sheltering in the basement.

The following night was much worse. The town was pounded by three waves of bombing by approximately 250 planes. When the exhausted and terrified people emerged from the shelters at 3.30 a.m. much the town was in ruins and the whole east end was burning.

Fortunately, after the first night's experience many families had fled the town to take refuge in the hinterland from Kilmacolm to Largs and beyond, so that casualties were much lighter than they would otherwise have been. Even so, 280 people were killed, and 1,200 injured.

St Lawrence's Church was on fire, and the priests and housekeeping staff were trapped as they sheltered in the heating chamber below the sacristy. The door, reached by an outside stair, was blocked with fallen rubble. With the church blazing furiously, a courageous parishioner, Mr Quigley, got them out by smashing a hole through the sacristy floor. "It is related that even at that critical time the Parish

1. J. L. Dow, op cit., p165.
2. Letter in possession of the author.

Priest took what is popularly called a dim view of this treatment of his beautiful sacristy floor"![1]

This Parish Priest was Canon William Horgan. a jovial but irascible Kerryman, who had been in charge of St Lawrence's since 1906. The new church had been opened only five years before his arrival, and he had painstakingly worked to complete the interior, with "marble side altars and pulpit, marble and bronze altar rails, superb oak panelling and fittings in the sacristy"[1] and, lastly, "the finest organ procurable in the country."[2] The organ had been installed and blessed only two months before it was burned to powder.

One of the curates, Fr O'Flynn, entered the blazing church to rescue the Blessed Sacrament, while firemen gave him what cover they could with their hoses. All three curates spent the rest of that dreadful night attending to the injured and dying.

The old Canon took refuge in a bus parked nearby and watched as his fine church was gutted.

The Franciscan Sisters offered Belltrees House to the priests as a temporary home, and they remained there until after the war.

* * *

Greenock continued to see plenty of evidence of the war at sea, as crippled ships limped or were towed into the Clyde for repair by the "black squads" who worked round the clock.

Church life was affected in unexpected ways — Midnight Mass was not celebrated at Christmas because of blackout regulations. On Holy Thursday morning, 1944, a priest from each of the Glasgow churches was invited to attend the Cathedral "to assist at the blessing of the Oils . . . We regret, however, that owing to the shortage of foodstuffs it will not be possible to provide breakfast for them this year."[3]

Great efforts were made to look after the servicemen who thronged the town. All during the war they climbed the stairs to the canteen run by the Catholic Women's League, in the flat above the paper shop in Grey Place. Many a romance blossomed over pie and chips, under the eagle eye of Miss Bridget Dunleavy.

Canon McMillan acted as Cupid on at least one occasion. Like the other clergy, he was conscientious in his care for the troops, often

1. John D. Canon Daniel, *St Peter's College Magazine*, December 1956.
2. *Glasgow Observer*, 2 July 1948.
3. Circular from Archdiocesan Office, 27 March 1944.

introducing them to families in the Parish by whom they were made welcome. He brought two Polish Naval officers to visit the home of Denis Murphy, a prominent parishioner, who ran a marine store in the town. Denis's daughter Alexandra was soon smitten by the handsome Josef Kuszynski, and they were married in 1942. "A fine romance", and just one of very many similar happy stories to lighten the wartime gloom.

(Alex Murphy was named after her uncle John, who became a Franciscan with the name of Fr Alexander. An artist, he made the drawing of St Mary's old church in East Shaw Street.)[1]

* * *

For those of us who did not experience the war it is hard to imagine what it must have been like. The more we read or see programmes about the war, the more we must admire the spirit that brought people through those dreadful years.

St Mary's Youth Club was formed in 1942, under the direction of Fr Francis McLeod. In the space of four years over fifty of its ex-members joined the Forces, a number claimed as a record among Youth Clubs in the district. 128 former pupils of St Mary's School who did not return are commemorated on the war memorial in the church. R.I.P. From these figures some inkling can be obtained of the high number of parishioners who served their country in the war.

Some who did return were broken in health, like Col. Hugh Kilpatrick, who as the senior British officer in his prisoner-of-war camp received the surrender of his Japanese captors.

On a lighter note, Private Benny Shields sent back an amusing account of his first day as a "rookie":

"TAR-RA-RA-RA-RA! 'My, my, the ice-cream man is out early to-day, or can it be the rag-man?' . . . I half-dressed (still in civvies) and walked sleepily into the washroom . . . I beheld a seething mass of humanity . . . there were five wash-hand basins between about two hundred men . . . I proceeded to wash myself. Imagine my surprise when the fellow next to me did it for me. One couldn't be sure whose face one was washing. I had to dry my face myself, since the said person was drying someone else's.

"After everyone had washed, shaved and got their own teeth back we were told to go to the dining hall for breakfast. . . The white fluid

1. See page 33

they called porridge . . . was so thin that you could tell whether the plate was cracked on the bottom or not . . . The coffee was grand except for the tea leaves which floated on top. I'm still trying to find out what we had for the rest of our meals. . .

"After breakfast we went for our first millitary parade, collecting our uniforms . . . My overcoat fitted me like a pair of gloves; it covered my hands. My boots were so big for me that when I started walking with them I had to take two steps before the boots left the ground . . ."[1]

Fortunately the war ended before Benny had to do any fighting.

* * *

Sunday 13 May 1945 was celebrated as a National Day of Thanksgiving for the end of the War. The 9.30 Mass was said "on behalf of the RAF, in thanksgiving, and for their fallen comrades."[2] The *Te Deum* was sung after the 12 o'clock Mass. Evening Devotions included the *De Profundis* for the souls of the fallen.

Three months later the celebration of VJ Day coincided with the Feast of the Assumption.

1. *St Mary's Youth Club Magazine*, 1946.
2. Notices Book, 1941-1945, St Mary's Archives.

St. Mary's Boys' Club Leaders

Chaplain—REV. T. MCKEOWN.

Supervisor—MR. J. WRIGHT.

Hon. President—MR. P. BRESLIN.

Woodwork.
Mr. P. Cuffe, Mr. A. Roberts, Mr. P. Carroll.

Gymnastics.
Mr. J. Wright, Mr. J. Canney, Mr. J. Wallace.

Electricity.
Mr. J. Orr.

Photography.
Mr. P. Breslin.

Entertainment.
Mr. I. Devine, Mr. D. Shields.

Choral Section.
Rev. T. McKeown.

Football Teams

Senior.
Mr. J. Wright, Mr. A. Roberts, Mr. J. Orr.

Junior.
Mr. H. Mullen, Mr. G. McLaughlin, Mr. A. Sutherland.

Football Coach—Mr. H. Cassidy.

JUNIOR BOYS' SECTION.

Mr. A. Sutherland.
Mr. J. Stewart.

BOYS' COMMITTEE.

President—Joe Stinson.

Treasurer—Jack McCue.

Secretary—Michael Docherty.

Members.
Wm. McVey, Pat Daisley, D. Carey, J. O'Hara, J. Callaghan, A. Scott, W. Sutherland, D. Shields, J. McAuley.

St. Mary's Girls' Club Leaders

Chaplain
REV. J. FISHER.

Supervisor
MISS M. MURPHY.

Dressmaking
MISS K. RICKETTS.

Leatherwork
MISS D. ROONEY.

Handwork
MISS M. GILLIGAN.

Music
MISS K. MCGURK.

Girls' Committee

Leader's Assistant:- MISS P. MULHERN.
W. DUNLOP, R. LAFFERTY, M. MCNELIS, A. MONTGOMERY, M. MCLAUGHLIN, R. CUMMINGS, C. CAMPBELL.

OFFICERS OF ST. MARY'S GROUP OF SCOUTS.

Group Scoutmaster—Mr. D. Thomson.

Assistants to 11th Troup of Scouts.
Mr. J. McCready, Mr. W. Gormley.

11th Cub Pack.

Cub Mistress.
Miss S. McDonald.

Assistant Cub Mistresses.
Miss J. Cook, Miss B. McGettigan.

Assistants to 54th Troup of Scouts.
Mr. J. Flanagan, Mr. A. Ward, Mr. S. Donnelly, Mr. J. Welsh.

54th Cub Pack.

Cub Mistress.
Miss M. Cannon.

Assistant Cub Mistress.
Miss J. Simpson.

Secretary and Treasurer—Mr. C. McCready.

Football Secretary—Mr. C. White.

Leaders of the Youth Club, 1946. ***From St Mary's Youth Club Magazine***

CHAPTER EIGHTEEN

The Post-War Years

GREAT sorrow was felt throughout the town at the unexpected death of Canon McMillan on 26 April 1945. On the following Sunday this announcement was read at all Masses:

"On Wednesday night at 8 o'clock Fr Cusick gave the last sacraments to the Canon — Absolution, Holy Viaticum and the Last Blessing. On Thursday the Rosary and the prayers for the dying were recited by all the priests of the house, and (by) the Canon's Staff and Relatives at 2 p.m., and the Canon died very peacefully in their midst at 3 o'clock.

"We beg your prayers that the Canon who lived so good a life may now receive from Our Lord the reward of a good life and happy death. He ministered to you for twenty-three years - gratitude and duty will ensure your prayers. May he rest in peace. Amen."[1]

On the day of his burial the road was lined with mourners all the way from Patrick Street to the Port Glasgow Boundary. All the children from St Mary's, St Mungo's and St Lawrence's schools were in the forefront.

Canon McMillan's successor was Canon William Horgan of St Lawrence's. Now in his eightieth year, he had been in poor health since his experience of the Blitz, and the subsequent difficult war years had taken their toll. He stayed at St Mary's less than two years before retiring to Ireland.

Canon Horgan gave 55 years' service to the Church in Scotland,

1. Notices Book 1941-1945, St Mary's Archives.

almost forty of them at St Lawrence's. Ordained at Maynooth in 1892 for his native Kerry, he was sent to Glasgow Archdiocese on loan, but soon sought permission to stay permanently. He ministered in Paisley, Houston and Stevenston before coming to Greenock, where he served on the Education Committee. He spent his retiral in the care of the Little Sisters in Cork, and he died there on 28 June 1948.

Canon William Horgan

He was sadly missed in Greenock, having been for so long a well-kent figure around the town, with his blackthorn stick and his Kerry Blue dog. He was known for his joviality and wit as well as for his sparky temper.

His dog was named Friday. Legend relates that when passing a building site, if the Canon thought the Catholic workmen were eating sandwiches with meat in them he would bellow, ostensibly to the dog, "Friday!"

* * *

During these years St Mary's Youth Club flourished, under the direction of its chaplains, Frs McLeod and Cusick, later succeeded by Frs McKeown and Fisher. The large membership enjoyed a wide range of activities, including camping, outings, sports and concerts. In 1946 the boys' section earned great praise for making a superb job of redecorating the Salon, which had been requisitioned by the Air Ministry during the war, and left in a dreadful state.

With the Salon refurbished, the Parish's social life could resume.

(Although we have been speaking of the "Parish", in fact it was not until 1946 that parishes were officially designated as such in the Archdiocese of Glasgow. Up until Canon Horgan's time the official title of the priest in charge was still "Missionary Rector".)

The new Parish Priest of St Mary's was Rev. Henry E. Hart, born in Dumbarton in 1895, the eldest of four brothers who all became priests. His studies were interrupted by the First World War, when he served with the artillery in France. He volunteered to join the Royal Flying Corps, but the war ended before he had finished his training. He went back to college, and was ordained in 1923.

His first posting was to Motherwell where he spent seventeen years before becoming Parish Priest of St Bride's, Bothwell, and then St Ninian's, Gourock. He was there for less than two years before being transferred to St Mary's.

Soon afterwards he was appointed Religious Inspector of schools

Fr Hart was a quiet, very unassuming man, of a retiring nature, but known for his generosity. His popularity can be gauged by the fact that several of his former parishioners from Motherwell attended his funeral in 1959, nearly twenty years after he had left them.

* * *

On 25 May 1947, with the Catholic population still rising, the Archdiocese of Glasgow was subdivided and the Dioceses of Paisley and Motherwell created by Pope Pius XII. St Mary's had been in the running to be the Cathedral Church of the new diocese, which comprised what was then the County of Renfrew. In the end St Mirin's, was chosen, and Greenock became part of the new Diocese of Paisley. The first Bishop was Rt Rev. James Black, consecrated on 14 April 1948.[1]

Coat of Arms of the Diocese of Paisley. St Mirin, patron of Paisley, is shown superimposed on a St Andrew's Cross, whose chequered design (blue and white) recalls the arms of the Stewarts, who were Barons of Renfrew, and founders of Paisley Abbey. The two shells recall St James the Greater, Paisley's other patron. The motto, "For the Good of Souls" is taken from the Apostolic Constitution of 1948 by which the diocese was created by Pope Pius XII. His crest — the dove of peace — is shown at the foot of the shield.

In Fr Hart's time the house and church were extensively refurbished and redecorated. New Sacred Heart and St Patrick's altars were erected, consecrated by Bishop William Andrew Hart of Dunkeld, Fr Hart's brother.

Fr Hart had a staunch ally in Mrs Mary Rennie (née Brennan), an outstanding benefactor of the church. Among her gifts were the new set of Stations of the

1. The Diocese of Paisley now comprises Renfrew and Inverclyde Districts.

Cross, the "Lourdes" window in memory of the Brennan Family, and the magnificent pipe organ, which is the glory of St Mary's.

Mrs Rennie donated prizes to all the local Catholic schools and to Glenburn Special School in which she took a great interest. Her generosity was legendary. Many still recall the splendour of the Forty Hours' Adoration in those days, when the Sanctuary was a blaze of candles, and filled to overflowing with the bowls of hyacinths which Mrs Rennie unfailingly provided for the occasion. The scent welcomed you as soon as you stepped in the door.

Reminiscing about his First Communion in 1946, Peter Mallon recalls that all the children received passes for the BB Cinema from Mrs Rennie.

Seven-year-old Peter must have looked cute in "white satin shirt, brown corduroy shorts (bought economically long), light blue silk ankle socks enclosed in brown sandals . . . It was one of the few occasions when . . . the youngest of four brothers, could expect a completely new outfit in the days of rationing of all kinds."[1]

Peter's nervousness on his First Communion Day was increased by the horror he felt as a child at the thought of stepping on the

Memorial slab marking the burial place in the vault of three great pastors of St Mary's: Dean Gordon, Canon Taylor and Canon Houlihan. ***Photograph by F. M. Dunlop***

1. Peter Mallon, unpublished article.

memorial tablet situated at that time on the floor at the end of the middle aisle, marking the burial vault. "This . . . had to be skirted with great care. What might happen if you did step on the stone was left shrouded in infantile dread."[1]

* * *

The Choir soared to great heights at this period, under the leadership of Willie Donnelly, organist and choirmaster extraordinary, who served St Mary's for over thirty years until shortly before his death in 1979. A brilliant musician with high standards of perfection, and a short fuse, he berated backsliding choristers in eloquent, but unecclesiastical language!

Under Willie's direction the Choir was considered one of the best in the Diocese, and was frequently heard on the radio, accompanied by the glorious tones of the organ.

St Mary's organ has quite a unique history. It was built[3] in 1886 for the Dixon Halls, Glasgow, where it remained until shortly before the First World War, when the Halls were refurbished. The organ was sold to a Glasgow organ builder, Andrew Watt, for a large house in Girvan. In 1949 the instrument was purchased for St Mary's, and installed with some modification.

"The organ casework was constructed by the German firm of E. F. Walcker of Ludwigsburg, before the First World War. It was never assembled, as it was caught at Glasgow Docks when war was declared. Later, after the War, (it was) sold at auction to Andrew Watt who used it as a façade (for St Mary's Church organ) in 1949. . .

"The organ is now (2001) one hundred and fifteen years old, containing historic pipework from one of the last Glasgow District Hall instruments. For insurance purposes, the present-day cost of building an organ of this size would be well over three hundred thousand pounds . . . (It) is soundly constructed and well worth looking after . . . a reliable and trustworthy instrument, well capable of another century of service in leading the praise."[3] A real treasure!

* * *

1. Ibid. When the Sanctuary was refurbished in the early 1960s the memorial tablet was replaced by a new one in front of the Altar.
2. By Joseph Brook of Busby.
3. Michael Macdonald (organ builder), unpublished article.

During the Fifties the population of the Parish continued to decline as the movement out to the new housing schemes increased. In 1950 the Parish numbered 3,900 souls; by 1962 the number had dropped to 3,500. For the first time the roll of St Mary's School dropped: in 1953 four teachers and 294 pupils were transferred to the new St Joseph's School; in 1957 ten teachers and 408 pupils to St Andrew's.

* * *

Fr Hart was in due course made a Canon of Paisley Chapter.

With quiet courage he accepted the diagnosis of an aortic aneurism, a condition for which in those days there was no treatment. For some time he was forced to be less active, "happily accepting little car outings with local colleagues".[1]

Canon Hart

Aged 63, he died very suddenly on 26 October 1959, while on a visit to his friend Fr Robert Barclay at St Joseph's.

"It was by all accounts the most impressive funeral in living memory in Greenock."[1] In the presence of Bishop Black and Bishop McGee of Galloway, Solemn Pontifical Requiem Mass was celebrated by Bishop Hart of Dunkeld; the deacon and subdeacon were the Canon's other brothers, Fr Andrew, a Cistercian from Nunraw, and Fr Gerard Hart, Parish Priest of Balornock. Around 150 priests attended, and a choir of priests was directed by Fr Barclay.

Once again the streets were lined by a guard of honour of schoolchildren, not only from St Mary's, but also St Mungo's and St Lawrence's.

Canon Hart is commemorated by a plaque at the Sacred Heart altar, its position in an unobtrusive corner of the church befitting the self-effacing nature of the man.

* * *

1. *Catholic Directory*, 1960.

Soon word came that the new Parish Priest was to be Canon John Daniel. A native of Shotts, he was ordained in 1923, on the same day as Canon Hart. (Canon Hart was a few years older than the usual age for ordination because of his war service.)

Fr Daniel served as curate in Dumbarton, where he was remembered for putting on concerts and operettas; then St Michael's, Parkhead, before being sent as Parish Priest to Strathaven. He was transferred to St Ninian's, Gourock, in 1944, where he interested himself in the welfare of the many sailors based in the area.

In 1945 he was appointed to St Lawrence's where the loss of the church had caused serious disruption to Parish life. A formidable character, Fr Daniel was equal to the challenge, giving strong leadership at a time of great difficulty. His crowning achievement was the opening of the new church in 1954. He remained at St Lawrence's for a further five years before being posted to St Mary's.

His intellectual gifts were of a high order. "He retained a lifelong interest in matters philosophical and in the social teaching of the Church."[1] Made a Canon when Paisley Diocese was formed, he was a "trusted adviser of the newly-consecrated Bishop Black."[1] Later he

St Mary's interior, 1950, taken at the wedding of Harry Cooper and Betty McKelvie . . . Note the fine marble pulpit.

1. *Catholic Directory*, 1960.

was appointed Provost of the Cathedral Chapter, a title he used with some pride.

A forceful personality, St Mary's found him very different from the gentle Canon Hart.

* * *

Curates of St Mary's around this time were Fr Fisher, a kenspeckle figure on his motor-bike with his hat stuck precariously on the back of his head; newly ordained Fr Duffin, who did his rounds by bicycle. And then there was Fr Molony.

How to convey just what Fr Molony meant to St Mary's? In the twenty-five years he spent in Greenock, "the old man with the stick", as he called himself, was probably the best-known and best-loved character in town.

Fr. Molony.
Photo by Rev B. J. Canning

And he was a character! Stories of Fr Molony abounded. Like the time police were holding up the traffic to let the Orange March pass along Union Street, but stopped the procession to let Fr Molony cross the road. He imperturbably dispensed blessings to right and left with his usual "God bless you, child!" (So the story goes!)

To go anywhere with Fr Molony was a protracted business, as everybody wanted to talk to him, and he stopped to talk to everybody, patting them on the head, young and old alike: "God bless you, child!" Loved by those of all denominations and none, he was an embodiment of ecumenism before it had a fancy name. He would have called it Christian charity.

He radiated holiness; he preached passionately on the love of God; he deeply influenced people just by loving them.

Quintessentially Irish (his party-piece was "The West's Awake"),

Fr Molony was born in Dublin (in a year he was never willing to divulge), and brought up by a Catholic father and Northern Protestant mother in a home which was so happy that he often referred to it as "heaven on earth". He entered the Cistercian Order and was ordained in 1922 at Mount St Bernard's Abbey, Leicester.

During the Second World War he volunteered to work outside the monastery, as there was a shortage of priests when so many had gone as chaplains to the Forces. He greatly enjoyed parish work in Nottingham, where much of his time was spent working with servicemen.

By 1950 he was suffering so severely from a stomach ulcer that he was no longer able to continue the hard life of a Cistercian monk. Since he had friends in Greenock he made application to Bishop Black, and was accepted for service in Paisley Diocese.

His tall, stooped, ascetic figure soon became known everywhere. He was always on the go, never off duty, visiting the hospitals, Gateside Prison, the homes of the sick . . . Under his gentle exterior was a shrewd mind, and a mischievous sense of fun. (He could do a brilliant take-off of his Parish Priest!)

Once ensconced in St Mary's his health improved, and gradually he began to look less ascetic!

A ST MARY'S LEGEND

I am not prepared to vouch for the truth of this story, but this is how I heard it!

Jimmy Stinson was for many years the janitor of St Mary's Patrick Street School. A dedicated worker, once a year he rigged up a cradle to hoist himself up to the top of the building to paint Our Lady's statue.

He also did odd jobs about the church. One time he decided that the near-life-size crucifix at the back of the church needed some attention — a couple of minor repairs, a lick of paint. It would be more convenient to work in his cubby-hole over at the school, so one dark winter's night he detached the crucifix from the wall and hoisted it on his shoulder to carry it up to the school.

It happened that just then a drunk man was weaving his way along Houston Street. At the corner he suddenly encountered this figure carrying a cross!

The drunk uttered an exclamation that was quite religious, and fled as fast as his unsteady legs would carry him, no doubt to swear off the drink after his "vision"!

Dinner in the Lorne Restaurant, celebrating the Golden Jubilee of St Mary's Higher Grade School, 1959. Headmaster Henry J. Kilpatrick is fifth from left at the top table, between Bishop Black and Provost Reid. How many other faces can you recognise?

First Communion at the Franciscan Convent, with Fr Hart, Sister Sebastian and Sister Chrysostom.

Pupils of Glenburn School, with Fr Fisher, Mrs Frances Dunlop and Miss Kathleen Murphy.

CHAPTER NINETEEN

Canon Daniel "A Man of Much Consequence"

THE centenary of the opening of the church was due to be celebrated in 1962. To mark the occasion Canon Hart had planned further decoration - mosaics for the Sanctuary was one thought in his mind. Canon Daniel had ideas on a much more grandiose scale.

What he wrote about the old St Lawrence's church applied equally to St Mary's: "Like most other churches of that period . . . the Sanctuary was too small and the Altar was rather dwarfed by the ornate reredos, giving the impression that the design of the Sanctuary was related more to Benediction than to the Holy Sacrifice of the Mass."[1]

Canon Hart's funeral had proved that there was not enough space in the Sanctuary to give dignity to really big celebrations, like the impending centenary.

Almost as soon as the new Parish Priest arrived he set about having the Sanctuary enlarged and raised.

Liturgically he was correct, of course; it was just unfortunate that the style of the period was so much at odds with the architecture of the church!

However, in the new, spacious Sanctuary the Solemn High Mass *coram episcopo*[2] for the 100th "birthday" of St Mary's church could

1. *St Peter's College Magazine* , 1956.
2. *In the presence of the Bishop.*

be celebrated with due solemnity, on the Feast of the Assumption, 15 August 1962. The following Sunday the Bishop sent his congratulations to "all concerned with last Wed's function — with a special word to the Choir."[1]

On 12 September, the Feast of the Holy Name of Mary[2] the church was consecrated by Bishop Black in an impressive ceremony. To be solemnly consecrated a church building must be free of debt, and St Mary's was at long last in that happy position.

The crosses round the church mark the spots where the walls were anointed by the Bishop with Oil of Chrism as a sign that this building is permanently devoted to the service of God. The twelve consecration crosses are a reference to the vision in the Book of Revelation of the Heavenly Jerusalem, with twelve gates, "and over the gates were written the names of the twelve tribes of Israel".[3]

Canon Daniel

The official Centenary celebration took place on Sunday 23 September, with a Solemn Pontifical Mass in the presence of Archbishop Campbell of Glasgow and Bishops Hart (Dunkeld), McGee (Galloway), and Ward (Auxiliary of Glasgow).

The Parish continued to celebrate with a Dinner and Dance, held on 9 October in the Lorne Restaurant in West Blackhall Street. Tickets cost 21/- (*£1.05p*).

* * *

1962 also saw the opening of the Second Vatican Council, which has had such far-reaching effects on the Church. The very first document issued was the *Constitution on the Sacred Liturgy*. As its implications began to be worked out the most obvious changes were the use of English which was gradually introduced into the Liturgy over

1. Notices Book 1962, St Mary's Archives.
2. Before the revision of the Liturgical Calendar.
3. Rv 21:12.

the next few years; and a return to the ancient practice of the priest facing the people while celebrating Mass. In St Mary's, as in most other churches, a temporary wooden altar was used meantime.

A new, larger porch was formed at the back of the church — very welcome as it cut the draughts!

* * *

"Like many men of strong character and convictions, Canon Daniel aroused many different reactions in different people . . . He could always be relied upon for a trenchant and perceptive comment on the affairs of the day. There was nothing he liked better than an argument, and many people will recall his way with words."[1] Indeed, his sermons, delivered in that rumbling bass voice, were always pithy and thought-provoking.

Canon Daniel was a perfectionist who did not suffer fools gladly. Woe betide the altar-boy who made the slightest slip-up. But behind his craggy and rather forbidding appearance, was much kindliness, a great zeal for souls, and even a scholarly sense of humour.

He was a popular after-dinner speaker, particularly at the Angling Club, of which he was a keen member.

The Canon was a passionate worker for inter-church friendship, doing at an official level what Fr Molony was doing at the grass roots. He was prominent in local affairs. His great friend, Rev. James

Fr James Fisher was an enthusiastic chaplain to the Legion of Mary. He is pictured at a Legion re-union. Left to right: Rose Lafferty, Kathleen Haggerty, Winnie Dunlop, Anne Clisham, Fr Fisher, Kathleen Alford, Eileen Feen, Margaret McKirdy, Cath McCabe and Joan Mooney.

1. *Catholic Directory*, 1973.

L. Dow, minister of Cartsburn-Augustine Church calls him "a man of much consequence in the town."[1]

He was justly proud of his part in drawing up "A Code for the Citizen" in 1950, during his time at St Lawrence's. This was a first for towns in Great Britain, and a remarkable (for the time) example of cooperation. It is reproduced at the end of this chapter, as perhaps it still has some relevance for us more than fifty years later.

The document was signed by Provost Robert Boyd, Rev. Alex V. Smart, Moderator of the Presbytery, Rev. John Young, President of the Greenock Ministers' Council, and Canon Daniel, representing the Catholic clergy of the town.

Rev. Dow concedes that "the cynic might remark that this Code has made little difference, . . . but it is greatly to the credit of the remarkable burgh which is Greenock, and with a Roman Catholic population almost as large as the Protestant population, and with a very strong Irish element, that it should have conceived and produced a document of such sense and vision."[1]

While one must be wary of making comparisons with other places, it is undeniable that such a population mix could have been an explosive recipe. That it was generally not so in Greenock must certainly be attributed in part to the quality of leadership given by the clergy, both Catholic and Protestant. This is not meant to sound self-congratulatory, or to claim that bigotry and prejudice (on both sides) did not exist; but the evidence does suggest that Greenock has a comparatively good record in this respect.

* * *

The Sixties saw changes taking place in the schools.

In 1967 the Convent School closed its doors, 93 years after the Franciscan Sisters set up their "middle-class school for day scholars".

The following year (1968) all staff and pupils from Captain Street and East Shaw Street, and Primary boys from Patrick Street, were transferred to the new school opened at Broomhill, under the Headship of Sister Sebastian who had succeeded Sister Theresa in 1950. "The school name was changed to St Patrick's, since the building was within that parish, and also to lessen the confusion with St Mary's Junior Secondary School in Patrick Street."[2] As long ago as 1930

1. James L. Dow, op. cit. p196.
2. *St Patrick's School Centenary Booklet.*

concern had been expressed by Inspectors over the suitability of the old East Shaw Street building! Only now were sufficient funds available to remedy the situation.

In the same year Glenburn Special School moved from Forsyth Street to its new premises on Inverkip Road. Until then, while the school was in St Mary's Parish, Fr James Fisher, and later Fr John McElroy were devoted chaplains to the Catholic pupils of Glenburn.

A big shake-up in secondary education was getting under way, with the introduction of the comprehensive system. In 1971 the great flitting took place from Peat Road to the new St Columba's, Bayhill, the first purpose-built six-year comprehensive school in Renfrewshire.

1971 was also the year we wrestled with the new decimal currency, trying to make sense of prices like £1.45 for a man's shirt, and 85p for boys' school shoes!

* * *

Canon Daniel was by now 72, and his health had been deteriorating for some time. His balance was affected and he had difficulty walking, latterly requiring help to struggle up and down the altar steps. But he was determined to continue saying Mass, and it was during Mass that he collapsed, dying in Larkfield Hospital early the next morning, 28 January 1972.

The principal celebrant at his Requiem was his elder brother, Canon Joseph Daniel of St Andrew's Cathedral, Glasgow. Present were Bishop McGill of Paisley, and Archbishop Scanlan of Glasgow with his two auxiliaries, Bishops Ward and Winning.[1] "In spite of the snow and intense cold, it was a packed church."[2]

Later in the year Fr Hugh Gallagher took up his appointment as Parish Priest of St Mary's.

1. Later Cardinal.
2. *Catholic Directory*, 1973.

A CODE FOR THE CITIZEN

We, the Provost, Magistrates and Councillors of the Burgh of Greenock, the Ministers of Religion, Protestant and Roman Catholic, address you in the interests of our common citizenship.

Every citizen derives great benefit from community life. Each citizen owes a debt to the community. A Christian civilisation especially is based on respect for the rights and well-being of others, and our civilisation is Christian in origin, history, principle and fact.

Crime, lawlessness, and malicious damage are obvious evils in our communal life. Less obvious, but no less distressing, is the attitude of those whose only aim is to get as much and to give as little as they can. There are some who just do not care. There are others who set the interest of one section above that of the whole. Our defects arise unmistakably from a denial of Christian morality in principle and practice. Without a return to Christian foundations there can be no ultimate remedy.

We therefore affirm the obligations of all citizens,

IN THE HOME:

— to accept the responsibilty of ensuring that community life is improved by our example;
— to live temperately;
— to spend wisely;
— to exercise toleration and patience in training children to be loyal, reverent, and well-mannered as members of a Christian nation;

A new generation in time will grow up to honour and respect parents whose whole interest has been the future of their children.

IN THE COMMUNITY AND AT WORK:

— to share in protecting public and private property;
— to respect the beauty and dignity of our town;
— to take an intelligent interest in the affairs of town and nation so that wise counsels and just laws may prevail;
— to seek to use our talents and concentrate interest on the job in hand.

All honest work is a contribution to the greater well-being of mankind.

IN SPIRITUAL MATTERS:

— to be completely sincere about our religious convictions and practices and at the same time to be tolerant of others who conscientiously differ from us;

As members of a Christian civilisation, we recognise that all authority, parental, civic, or religious, is from God, and the society that ignores or dishonours God, the source of all goodness, must inevitably deteriorate.

CHAPTER TWENTY

Monsignor Gallagher "Fifty Years of Loyal Service"

BORN in Clydebank in 1920, Rev. Hugh Gallagher was ordained in St Andrew's Cathedral, Glasgow in 1945.

His first appointment was to St Ninian's, Gourock, where he spent eleven years before being sent as Vice-Rector to the Royal Scots College, Valladolid. After seven happy years in Spain he was recalled to Scotland, spending a few months at St Thomas's, Neilston, before being appointed full-time chaplain to the Little Sisters in Greenock. There followed a brief spell as priest-in-charge of St Joseph's and St Patrick's, Wemyss Bay, until in 1969 he became the first Parish Priest of St Columba's, Renfrew, where he oversaw the building of the new church.

Three years later he was transferred to the "Grand Old Lady of Patrick Street", as he was fond of calling St Mary's.

* * *

1972 also saw the arrival of the Sisters of the Sacred Heart of Mary, who in their sixteen years here made such a great contribution to the life of the district. To alleviate the desperate shortage of teachers at that time Bishop McGill sought help from religious congregations in England. A house was provided at 85 Finnart Street, and five S.H.M. Sisters moved in. Their first Superior was Sister Kevin, who although past retirement age went to augment the Catholic teaching staff at Glenburn. The other Sisters taught in various local schools, and one worked as a nurse.

"Like all projects the beginnings were difficult, not least understanding the Scottish dialect." (Most of the Sisters were Irish.) "The people were very welcoming and hospitable. Fr Gallagher and Fr Logue were very helpful in introducing us to the parish."[1]

The Sisters soon undertook a wide variety of pastoral work, particularly visiting the elderly and housebound. They were involved with the Legion of Mary, S.V.D.P., Justice and Peace, and collaborated with Fr Joseph Logue in establishing a prayer group. In the wider area Sisters were involved in Greenock Council of Churches, took Sunday School at Wemyss Bay, worked with St Lawrence's Youth Club, and with the girls at the Good Shepherd Convent, Bishopton.

The Sisters remained until 1988, by which time "there was a surplus of teachers in the area and our missions in Zambia and Brazil were making urgent demands on personnel in the Province. Feeling that our work in Greenock had been accomplished, in consultation with Bishop Mone it was decided to withdraw the Sisters from Greenock. Bishop Mone assisted by Bishop McGill celebrated a Mass of thanksgiving . . . A lively evening of music and song was a fitting completion to a happy venture in Scotland."[1]

Fr Gallagher and Bishop McGill at the opening of the Loreto Club in 1974. Others in the picture are (l. to r.): Kathleen Stewart, Maureen Quigley, Rose Barry, Joe Stewart, William Barry, Joe Bain and Gerry Quigley.
Photograph by James Hall

1. Sister Eleanor Dalton, unpublished article.

The Sisters left behind many friends, by whom they were greatly missed. Who could forget seeing Sister Assumption and Sister de Lourdes walking down to St Mary's together, the one so tall and the other so tiny!

* * *

Soon after his arrival at St Mary's in 1972 Fr Gallagher was greatly perturbed that there was no longer a school in the Parish. The boys from Patrick Street and the girls from Loreto[1] were transferred in a massive operation to the refurbished former St Columba's building in Peat Road. In its new incarnation as a comprehensive the school was renamed Notre Dame. Primary pupils had of course already been moved to St Patrick's.

The historic school building in Patrick Street lay empty, and was destined to be converted to Council offices.

On the very day he was due to take up his new appointment at St Paul's, Foxbar, Fr John McElroy deputised for Fr Gallagher at a meeting with the Provost and town councillors. He eloquently made the case for retaining a school in at least part of the building, sketching its importance as a monument to the past, not only for Catholics, but for the whole town. The building had been erected, not with public money, but with "the pennies of the poor". Protestants as well as Catholics had contributed.

Fr Gallagher held meetings with parents and officials, and, assisted by an dedicated committee of parishioners, campaigned tirelessly for a school, realising how important it was for the vitality of the Parish.

His case was helped by the fact that St Patrick's School was soon full; the school-age population of St Mary's Parish was increasing. Yes, a new school was necessary. Rather than a new building being erected, Fr Gallagher advocated the refurbishment of the old school which had so much tradition built into its solid old walls. Eventually this course was adopted, and in 1975 St Mary's Primary School opened its doors, under its first Head Teacher, Mrs Marie Hagan. 186 pupils and four teachers were transferred from St Patrick's to the new school.

* * *

1. The Loreto Club in Houston Street, opened in 1974, perpetuates the name of the old school.

Franciscan Centenary Mass, 9th February, 1974. The photograph shows the alterations to the sanctuary which took place in the 1960s. A temporary wooden altar was still in use.

Meanwhile, in 1974 the Franciscan Sisters whose community at this time numbered six, celebrated the centenary of their arrival in Greenock. Like the S.H.M. Sisters, the Franciscans had always played an active part in local life: "Over and above teaching in the schools the Sisters visit the poor, the aged and lonely as well as the sick in the local hospitals; instruct converts; teach music and conduct a girls' club. Another aspect of the social work undertaken by the Sisters has always been the visiting of the women and young offenders in Gateside Prison."[1]

* * *

Under Fr Gallagher, who was installed as a Canon in 1975, the remodelling of the Sanctuary continued, in line with Vatican II liturgical reforms. A new altar replaced the temporary one. The baptismal font was moved to the Sanctuary and the baptistery was converted to St Theresa's shrine. Controversially, the pulpit was demolished and replaced by a lectern.

The Choir was disbanded about this time, in an attempt to foster congregational singing, in line with the directives of the Council. Fr Logue was indefatigable in his efforts to coax us to sing! For centuries Catholic congregations had been deprived of their voice, while the choir did all the work! It was hard to convince us to reclaim our rightful place in the Liturgy!

* * *

1975 saw the end of an era when Fr Molony retired in September, slipping away quietly to avoid any fuss. The *Telegraph* quoted Fr Gallagher: "People have been coming up to me all week and asking me if it is true he has gone for good . . . The house, like the town, is empty without him."[2]

Fr Joseph Logue left St Mary's at the same time. Canon G.N.Pennie, Rector of St John's Episcopal Church, wrote a tribute to both of them in his parish magazine:

"I cannot end this letter without mentioning the departure from Greenock to Dublin of Father Molony, and Father Logue's departure to Johnstone where he is now parish priest. Father Molony's great

1. *A Cause for Rejoicing — One Hundred Years in Greenock.* (Centenary booklet)
2. *Greenock Telegraph*, 11 September 1975.

love for all people, no matter their faith or lack of it, has endeared him to hundreds, and possibly thousands, during his twenty-five years in Greenock. We wish him a long and happy retirement. Father Logue was a very sympathetic and friendly man who will be missed by many, and we congratulate him on his promotion."[1]

Fr Molony was cared for by the Little Sisters in Dublin until his death in February 1978. He was in his eighties, but would have been amused by the fact that newspaper reports of his death gave contradictory reports of his age, a detail about which he was very secretive!

* * *

On 1 July 1978 a capacity congregation witnessed a historic event as Fr Peter McGarry was ordained to the priesthood by Bishop McGill. This was the first ordination ever to take place in St Mary's, as the previous practice had been for priests to be ordained in the Cathedral. Fr Peter is currently (2001) Parish Priest of St Charles', Paisley.

Fr Peter McGarry, whose ordination in 1978 was the first to take place in St Mary's Church.
Photograph: Greenock Telegraph

So far, three more priests have been ordained in St Mary's Church: Rev. Brian McGee (1989), now Parish Priest of St Joseph's, Clarkston; Rev. Richard Hagan C.SS.R., and Rev. Richard Reid C.SS.R. The fact that the two latter joined the Redemptorists bears testimony to the long-standing link between that Order and St Mary's. Redemptorists have been conducting parish missions here for well over a century. They promoted the Novena to Our Lady of Perpetual Succour which was a feature of the devotional life of the Parish for many years.[2]

* * *

1. *St John's Parish Magazine*, 6 October 1975.
2. Another ordination of a parishioner in recent years was that of Fr Stephen O.S.B. (Colin Geddes), which took place at Fort Augustus Abbey in 1988.

Canon Gallagher was a keen pilgrimage-goer, and led Parish groups, notably to Lourdes, Rome and Iona. And to Bellahouston on that unforgettable day in 1982 when Pope John Paul II visited Scotland.

In 1984 it was the turn of the Little Sisters to celebrate their centenary. Bishop McGill wrote: "By your wonderful and constant goodness you have merited the eternal gratitude of your aged guests, and the profound esteem and thanks of the community at large."[1]

* * *

When Bishop Stephen McGill retired in 1988, Canon Gallagher was honoured with the title of Monsignor, in recognition of his years of efficient service as diocesan treasurer.

A member of the National Liturgy Commission, Monsignor Gallagher was always abreast of current thinking, as liturgical reform progressed following the directives of the Second Vatican Council. He encouraged the formation of the lay ministries, appointing readers, and Eucharistic Ministers. He ensured that St Mary's was in the forefront of liturgical development. For instance, St Mary's was one of the first churches in the Diocese to introduce the ministry of cantor, at the behest of the new Bishop John Mone. Monsignor cared deeply about liturgy, and had very decided views on what was fitting.

* * *

A cause for concern was the lack of a Parish Hall, since the old Salon had been sold off in Canon Daniel's time to finance the alterations to the church. At last Monsignor was able to set about a long-cherished project to build a new hall next to the church. At its opening on 18 March 1994 the Loreto Singers provided a sparkling entertainment of Irish songs.

Sadly, Monsignor suffered a stroke the following May, which led to his retiral later in the year.

There was now a complete change of personnel at St Mary's, with Fr Dow and Fr Sheridan both being transferred, and Fr Paul Cosh being appointed as assistant priest.

He arrived in October 1994, a week before the new Parish Priest, Fr Andrew Carroll.

1. Rev B.J. Canning, *Instruments of His Work* (Centenary booklet).

In June the following year parishioners were delighted that Mgr Gallagher was well enough to return to St Mary's to celebrate his Golden Jubilee. After Mass, which Monsignor concelebrated with Bishop John Mone, Bishop Stephen McGill, and a number of priest friends, Fr Andrew hosted a Parish lunch in the beautiful new hall.

A few days later a group of parishioners travelled to Glasgow to take part in the Mass which Monsignor concelebrated in St Andrew's Cathedral with three of his classmates who were ordained there with him in 1945.

Monsignor Gallagher was President of Inverclyde Voluntary Association for Mental Health, a cause dear to his heart. He is remembered for his devoted attention to the sick of the Parish, and his kindness and compassion towards the bereaved. As senior priest in the Diocese he was Provost of the Cathedral Chapter.

"I believe that among his many achievements it is Mgr Gallagher's 50 years of loyal service to the Diocese and the Church in Scotland which is his greatest achievement," said Bishop John Mone, paying tribute to Monsignor on his retirement.[1]

James Deegan makes a presentation to Mgr Gallagher for his Golden Jubilee.

1. *Greenock Telegraph*, 22 September 1994.

CHAPTER TWENTY-ONE

Rev. Andrew Carroll "The Million Pound Man"

WHEN it became known that Fr Andrew Carroll was to be in charge of St Mary's, many people said, "Who?" His previous record was not such as to make him widely known in the Diocese.

Andrew Carroll, from Barrhead, followed a career in nursing before deciding to study for the priesthood. After ordination in 1974 his first posting was to St Mary's, Paisley, where he spent thirteen years. He was then sent to St Patrick's, Greenock, for a year, before being appointed Director of St Vincent's Centre in Langbank. (The former premises of St Vincent's College were used for some years as a retreat and conference centre.)

There followed a year of study at Gonzaga University in Washington State, then a year of parish work in California. Although tempted to remain in the sunshine, in the end the pull of home was too strong. He returned to Scotland in 1994, and soon afterwards was appointed to St Mary's. He made an immediate good impression: as with his predecessor, Canon Taylor, his homilies "never failed to convey a vast amount of instruction within a small compass."[1]

The Parish House was in need of upgrading and modernisation, and one of Fr Andrew's first tasks was to undertake a programme of refurbishment.

1. *Catholic Herald*, January 1905.

* * *

By this time it was apparent that vocations to the priesthood were not so plentiful as in former times.

With great wisdom and foresight Fr Andrew addressed this situation shortly after his arrival. He pointed out that this was a problem likely to become acute in the future. St Mary's formerly had four or five priests, and now had only two. He foresaw a time when it would not be possible to take for granted that there would be even one priest for each parish. The future of the Parish depended on the laity playing their full part.

Things were changing in the Church, but it could be seen as a time of opportunity rather than crisis. It was Fr Andrew's stated intention to begin training his people to take responsibility for their own Parish.

Fr Andrew's American experience was of great relevance as the Church there had faced the same problem of dwindling numbers of clergy.

In his own unique style, Fr Andrew fostered greater lay involvement in the running of the Parish. At his happiest when working as part of a team, he soon surrounded himself with an army of willing workers. He had a great knack of finding the right person for the job.

The already-existing lay ministries were expanded; Children's Liturgy was introduced; and the Parish Council was set up in 1995 as directed by the Bishop. One of Fr Andrew's innovations was the Welcoming Ministry, with the important remit of ensuring that no-one feels a stranger as we gather for Sunday worship. The Choir was re-formed, first under Joyce Coyle, and later under Gregory McHugh, who was appointed Director of Music in 1999,[1] a post he held until July 2001. The Youth Group, led by Sean Linning, also provided music for some of the Masses.

As part of his "master plan" to bind the Parish community closer together, Fr Andrew encouraged more social activity, aided by an enthusiastic Social Committee. From now on it was "any excuse for a party" — mince pies and mulled wine after Christmas Midnight Mass, pancakes on Shrove Tuesday, tea and buns after 10 o'clock Mass on the Feast of the Assumption, St Patrick's dances, Burns

1. It is worth noting that in the post-Vatican II Church, the function of the Choir has changed. The main Ministers of Music are the Priest and People, who unite in singing the Liturgy (not just hymns!). The function of the Cantor is to lead the Assembly in sung prayer, and to facilitate the people's response. Choir, organ, and other musicians serve to enhance the Liturgy, but primarily to support the singing of the Assembly.

Suppers . . . Particularly happy occasions were the "pot luck" lunches, with everyone contributing a different dish. On such occasions Father would remark, "This is the Parish at its best."

Fr Andrew's warmth and humanity touched everyone. His great gift to St Mary's was to weld us into a true family community.

After Fr Paul's departure in 1996, St Mary's became a one-priest parish. With his cheerful manner Fr Paul was a breath of fresh air, and his smiling face was much missed.

* * *

Having worked hard to build up the "living stones" of the Church, Fr Andrew now turned his attention to the crumbling stones of St Mary's building. It was obvious that urgent and drastic action was needed to carry out repairs.

For example: One rainy morning during 10 o'clock Mass Father had just said: "Lord, wash away my iniquities and cleanse me from my sins", when a splash of water from the roof landed on his head! A dramatic answer to prayer, perhaps, but certainly a further sign that renovation was a number one priority.

Another example: During the Vigil Mass one Saturday evening, a loud crack was heard, and the people in the side aisle were showered with debris from the roof.

Emergency repairs were carried out on the roof beams. Plans were set in motion for major repairs and refurbishment of the church. A Steering Group was set up. In January 1999 Fr Andrew boldly launched an appeal for £1 million. 2002 was chosen as a target date, this being the 140th anniversary of the opening of the church.

* * *

In June 1999 Fr Andrew celebrated the Silver Jubilee of his Ordination. After Mass and a presentation in the church a buffet lunch was enjoyed in the Hall.

The following September St Mary's School suffered a great upheaval when serious structural damage was found in the building. The authorities acted with commendable speed, closing down the school immediately and getting repairs under way.

Temporary accommodation was found for staff and pupils at St Columba's, Bayhill, until the following April, when they were able to move back to Patrick Street, confident that the building would not fall down around them.

At the end of the year 1999 the Franciscan Sisters moved out of "Glenlea" along the road to a smaller house at 54 Newark Street.

A few weeks later two of the Sisters celebrated the Golden Jubilee of their Profession: Sr Therese (the Parish's Pastoral Assistant) and Sr Helena.

Fr Andrew Carroll, wth parishioners Katie Couper, Sheila MacMillan and Margaret Garvie, launching the million pound Building Fund Appeal in January, 1999. ***Photograph: Greenock Telegraph***

* * *

In the year 2000 the Church throughout the world celebrated the Great Jubilee. In preparation for Easter in this special year two Redemptorist Fathers gave a Mission in St Mary's during Lent.

As the Mission drew to a close, all were stunned when it became known that Fr Andrew had suffered a heart attack.

Many were the heartfelt prayers offered for his return to health, but although he recovered, he was not fit enough to return to parish duties, and in September he tendered his resignation to the Bishop.

During the months of Father Andrew's illness the team spirit and sense of community he had built up helped the Parish through a difficult time.

We were fortunate that two retired priests were living in the Parish: Canon Andrew Reid, former Parish Priest at Wemyss Bay, and Fr Joseph Logue, former Parish Priest of Bishopton, who had spent six years as a curate in St Mary's in the 1970s. We owe a great debt to them and to Sister Therese for maintaining the sacramental life of the Parish.

* * *

On 10 June a large crowd joined with the Hierarchy of Scotland for the National Celebration of the Great Jubilee, at the Courier Stadium, Livingston. A spectacular pageant was followed by Mass, at which one of the cantors was Gemma Coyle, a young parishioner of St Mary's.

In September Fr John Tormey took up his appointment as Parish Priest. Soon afterwards he welcomed Fr Andrew back to St Mary's for a farewell presentation, a joyful-sad occasion, when all present shared very mixed feelings.

Fr Joseph Logue

Sister Therese

Canon Andrew Reid

Photographs by F. M. Dunlop.

Celebrating Fr Andrew's Silver Jubilee, June 1999.

The celebrations continue — above (left): Anne McElroy, of the Social Committee, casts an appraising eye over the "purvey" provided by parishioners for Fr Andrew's Silver Jubilee celebrations; and right: Winifred Bain and Greta McGowan, just two of the willing helpers in the kitchen for a Parish celebration. They don't look too overwhelmed by drudgery!

Photographs by F. M. Dunlop

First Communicants, St Mary's Primary School, 2000. ***Photographs by Tempest Photography.***

CHAPTER TWENTY-TWO

New Beginnings

DEAR Parishioners, I am Father John Tormey, and I am very happy to be your new parish priest. I look forward to meeting you in the coming weeks and months ahead. Please pray for me that I may do the Lord's work here in St Mary's with love and generosity of heart.

This is how Fr John introduced himself in the Parish Newsletter on 24 September 2000.

Fr John Tormey
Photograph by F. M. Dunlop

Born in Greenock, John Tormey was baptised in St Patrick's Church, later moving to St Andrew's Parish. He was educated at St Vincent's College, Langbank, St Mary's College, Blairs, and the Pontifical Scots College, Rome. He proudly recalls that during his holidays from college he worked at Ardyne Point, building oil-drilling platforms (not single-handedly — a few others helped, including his father!)

Fr John was ordained to the priesthood by Bishop McGill on 28 June 1981. This was the first ordination to take place in St Andrew's Church. After spending two years at St Mirin's, Paisley, Fr John was sent back to Rome to join the staff of Scots College. He remained at the College for eight years, six of them as Vice-Rector. While in Italy he was chaplain to Scouts, in the Parish of Santa Chiara, close to the College. (This was the late Cardinal Gray's titular church.)

On being recalled to Scotland Fr John spent three years at St Joseph's, Greenock. During this time he served as chaplain to the Ardgowan Hospice.

In 1995 he became Parish Priest of St Fergus', Paisley, a post he held for five years. He was also appointed diocesan treasurer, and until June 2001 he was a part-time lecturer in philosophy at Scotus College, Bearsden.

By this time the shortage of priests was beginning to be felt in the Diocese, and no priest was available to fill the vacancy in the neighbouring parish of St James.

The Daughters of Charity were asked to look after the pastoral care of the parish, and Fr John acted as Sacramental Administrator. It was a time, he says, when he "experienced a new form of team ministry which was very successful".

In September 2000, he returned to Greenock as Parish Priest of St Mary's.

When Fr John arrived at St Mary's he was in a sense coming home, as his mother came from a long-established St Mary's family. In fact his aunt, Agnes Gillespie, and his great-grandfather, John Gillespie, feature in the 1923 Choir photograph.

In his short time amongst us Fr John has shown himself to be a zealous and caring priest.

* * *

In October 2000 it was announced that the Little Sisters' Home in Union Street was to close for redevelopment. A new modern facility will be built on the same site, and it is hoped that the work of the Sisters will continue for many years to come.

The following February Bishop John came to celebrate Mass for the Silver Jubilee of St Mary's Primary School, established in the old building in 1975.

* * *

Fr John inherited the huge responsibility of leading the refurbishment programme. He found that great progress had been made in fundraising. In the first year since the launching of the Appeal £130,000 was raised from numerous moneymaking schemes, and many generous donations. This despite the fact that we have not tried some of the ideas of previous generations of St Mary's fundraisers. I wonder how successful a charity sermon would be nowadays! Or a Grand Washing Competition!

Fr John holds a print of the 1887 painting of St Mary's by Patrick Downie.

Photograph by Gerard Ralston

Martin McGeehan, who chaired the Steering Group for its first two years, pays tribute to "the splendid work of virtually all the Parish Ministries and many, many parishioners who immediately swung into action, raising funds and spreading news of our ambitious project. And it was ambitious. Around £1,300,000 would be needed to make the necessary repairs, some appropriate alterations, and set St Mary's on a sound footing to serve the local community for another 200 years . . .

"After some research on where similar projects might be found, friends at Greenock's own Wellpark Mid Kirk, and several church communities around the West of Scotland helped by explaining how they had set about the task . . . Local Councillors, MPs and MSPs, the *Greenock Telegraph*, Ardgowan School and a local Theatre Company were among those who wrote to encourage and support St Mary's . . .

"Parishioners put their shoulders to the wheel, devising fundraising schemes, to encourage others to put their hands in their pockets. It is virtually impossible to list them all . . .

"To mention just a few: the West Highland Way was walked, our Children's Liturgy saved 20 pence pieces, the Youth Group produced a CD, quiz nights, dances, fetes were held. The Social Committe, Loreto Club and other groups within the parish became involved in a stream of fundraising initiatives . . .

"Stunning, framed reproductions of the (Patrick Downie painting of St Mary's) were soon speeding their way to parishioners and their families and friends throughout the world . . .

"A Book of Dedication (was established), which allows parishioners, and friends from further afield to have a donation to the 2002 Project associated with a loved one . . .

"Paula and Rik Smith developed our *stmarysgreenock.org* website which takes news of the St Mary's 2002 project, and wider parish information, to friends of St Mary's from Thurso to Toronto, from Bournemouth to Brisbane. And it gives them the opportunity to donate online! . . .

"As the Parish entered 2001, and consultation with parishioners was taking place on detailed, final plans, tremendous progress had been made."[1] There is still a long way to go, but with fundraising well on track, and grants having been secured from Historic Scotland and the Heritage Lottery Fund, the project is set to proceed as planned.

1. Martin McGeehan, unpublished article.

Eddie Beattie, R.I.P., Sacristan 1991-2001
Photo by F. M. Dunlop

Work is scheduled to begin early in 2002. Once the structural repairs have been carried out, and the church has been made weather-tight, proposed alterations will make the interior look somewhat different. A new side entrance and office area will be made beside the Lady Chapel, on the site of the existing sacristy. A new sacristy will be formed from the present servers' sacristy and office/library. The rear porch will be remodelled, as will the Sanctuary, with a new altar and lectern being installed. These will incorporate the attractive marble rails currently in front of the side altars. There will be new lighting, heating and public address systems, and as a finishing touch, the exterior will be landscaped and floodlit.

By the time we celebrate our bicentenary in the year 2008 please God we will be well settled into our magnificently renovated church.

* * *

When Mr John Davidson arrived in 1808 to found the Greenock Mission he offered Mass in a hired hall for a congregation of about a hundred poor, displaced persons, Highlanders and Irish in the main. His "patch" was extensive, covering an area from Dunbartonshire to Ayrshire.

Almost two hundred years later St Mary's can proudly claim to be the "mother" of the many parishes which now flourish in this part of the West of Scotland.

The town has seen many changes over two centuries, with the rise and demise of the traditional industries of shipbuilding, sugar refining and heavy engineering, their place being taken by such things as electronics and call centres. Greenock is no longer a busy port, with only a few cruise ships and container ships calling in occasionally.

St Mary's Parish is now confined to the central and west parts of Greenock, stretching east-west from Cathcart Street to Eldon Street at the Gourock Boundary. In the year 2000 the Parish population was approximately 2,350, a figure which has remained fairly stable for the last forty years.

The Parish is a vibrant community, with many active organisations. Pride of place must go to the St Vincent de Paul Society which has been helping the local needy since 1855. As well as visiting hospitals and spending time with people in their own homes, St Mary's Conference is twinned with other conferences in India, Malta and South Africa.

The Legion of Mary, established in St Mary's in 1932, "participates in the life of the parish through visitation of families, the housebound, the sick at home or in Inverclyde Hospital, recitation of the Rosary in the homes of deceased parishioners, (and) in particular the promotion of Eucharistic Devotion and the Rosary."[1]

Other organisations include the Union of Catholic Mothers, Catholic Charismatic Renewal, RCIA, Baptism Ministry, SCIAF/Justice and Peace, Youth Music Group, Altar Society, Charities Group, and not least, the Social Committee. Some parishioners are involved in Inverclyde Churches Together to promote inter-church activity. (All these organisations would welcome new members.)

Worshipping in our venerable neo-Gothic church, we are a much more prosperous-looking bunch than our ancestors, very different in outlook in many ways. And yet underneath the outward appearances, we are just the same as they were, sharing a common bond of Faith.

In tracing our story we pay tribute to the gifted and sometimes heroic priests who have served us, and to our predecessors, the people of St Mary's who have handed down their Faith to us through the last two hundred years, persevering in spite of many difficulties.

We pray that by our attempts to live out the Gospel, and by our care for one another we, their descendants, may be messengers of God's love in our corner of Clydeside.

1. Parish Directory, 1998.

Ready to lead St Mary's into the future. Left to right: Scott Dyer, Gill Loftus, Michael Frizzel and Kevin Hendry. ***Photograph by F. M. Dunlop***

St Mary's interior in 2000. Apart from the shell of the building, nothing remains of the original 1862 church except the baptismal font, which can be seen on the right of the Sanctuary. Watch this space for further alterations, due to start in 2002. ***Photograph by Gerard Ralston***

APPENDIX 1

A CHRONICLE OF EVENTS

NOTE: M.R. = Missionary Rector
P.P. = Parish Priest *(Post-1946)*

1798	Abbé Capperon advertises French classes in Greenock.	Ch.2
1805	Death of M. Capperon. M. Lemonnier teaches French.	Ch.3
1808	**Greenock Mission established by Rev. John Davidson.**	Ch.4
1815	8 Jan: Death of John Davidson.	
	Rev. John Gordon M.R.	Ch.5
1816	**25 Aug: Opening of St Mary's Church, East Shaw Street.**	
1818	**11 Oct: Opening of St Mary's School.**	
1827	Greenock becomes part of new Western District.	
1829	**Catholic Emancipation Act.**	
1830	Dumbarton becomes an independent Mission.	
1833	Rev. John Gordon resigns.	Ch.6
1834	**Bishop Andrew Scott moves to Greenock.**	
1837	Gallery added to church.	
1840	8 Aug: Rev. Dr Peter Keenan dies of typhus.	
1846	Port Glasgow becomes an independent Mission.	Ch.7
	4 Dec: Death of Bishop Scott.	
1847	Aug: Rev. Dr Richard Sinnott dies of typhus.	
	Rev. James Danaher M.R.	
1850	- 1855 "Angel Gabriel" riots.	Ch.8
1852	**Rev. William Gordon M.R.**	
1855	12 Aug: Opening of St Lawrence's Chapel.	Ch.9
1859	St Lawrence's becomes an independent Mission.	
1862	**17 Aug: Opening of St Mary's Church, Patrick Street**	Ch.10
1867	Rev. Alexander Taylor arrives as curate.	Ch.11
1872	Education (Scotland) Act.	
1874	Franciscan Sisters arrive in Greenock.	Ch.12
	Convent School opens.	
1878	**4 March: Restoration of the Hierarchy**	
	2 Oct: Opening of new school, East Shaw Street.	
1880	Opening of Gourock Chapel-School.	
	15 Dec: Death of Dean Gordon.	
	Rev. Alexander Taylor M.R.	Ch.13

1884 Little Sisters of the Poor arrive in Greenock.
1890 Renovations : new High Altar.
1892 Fr Taylor's Silver Jubilee
1896 Gourock becomes an independent Mission.
1897 Dec: Bazaar for School.
Duncan St School purchased to accommodate boys.
1902 Rectory extended. Ch.14
1905 6 Jan: Death of Canon Taylor.
Rev. Patrick Houlihan M.R.
Aug: Fire in Girls' School, E. Shaw St. Ch.15
1907 Fr Houlihan's Silver Jubilee.
1909 **Opening of St Mary's Higher Grade School, Patrick Street.**
1912 Oct: Bazaar for School.
1913 Franciscan Sisters move to "Glenlea", Madeira St.
1914 - 1918 First World War.
1914 Major alterations to Church : new Lady Chapel, new Baptistery, new door in tower, electricity installed.
1918 Education (Scotland) Act.
1922 **Opening of Captain Street School.**
1923 4 Jan: Death of Canon Houlihan.
Rev. John McMillan M.R.
1924 12 Jan : Golden Jubilee of Franciscan Sisters.
St Patrick's Parish established.
1924 7 Dec: Dedication of Lady Altar built in memory of Canon Houlihan.
1933 16 June: Opening of St Columba's Secondary School.
1934 Golden Jubilee of Little Sisters.
1939 - 1945 Second World War Ch.17
1945 26 April: Death of Canon McMillan. Ch.18
V. Rev. William Canon Horgan M.R.
1946 Canon Horgan retires to Ireland.
Rev. Henry E. Hart P.P.
1947 **25 May: Diocese of Paisley formed.**
1959 26 Oct: Death of Canon Hart.
V. Rev. John D. Canon Daniel P.P. Ch.19
1962 Opening of Second Vatican Council.
1963 Sanctuary enlarged.
Centenary of church.
12 Sept: Consecration of church
1967 Franciscan Convent School closes.
1968 Opening of St Patrick's Primary School; all staff and pupils transferred from St Mary's, Captain Street and East Shaw Street; primary boys from Patrick Street.
1972 28 Jan: Death of Canon Daniel.
Rev. Hugh Gallagher P.P. Ch.20

1972 Opening of Notre Dame High School; all staff and pupils transferred from St Mary's, Patrick Street and Loreto.
Sacred Heart Sisters arrive.
1974 Centenary of Franciscan Sisters' arrival in Greenock.
1975 **Opening of St Mary's Primary School.**
Alterations to Sanctuary.
1982 1 & 2 June: Visit to Scotland of Pope John Paul II.
1984 Little Sisters' Centenary.
1988 Sacred Heart Sisters leave Greenock.
1994 18 March: Opening of St Mary's Hall.
Mgr Gallagher retires.
Oct: **Rev. Andrew Carroll P.P.** Ch.21
1995 June: Mgr Gallagher's Golden Jubilee.
Parish Council established.
1999 January: £1 million Appeal launched.
June: Fr Andrew's Silver Jubilee.
Franciscan Sisters move to 54 Newark St.
2000 10 June: National Jubilee Celebration, Livingston.
Sept: Fr Andrew retires.
Fr John Tormey P.P. Ch.22
Oct: Little Sisters' Home closes for redevelopment.
St Mary's website established: *stmarysgreenock.org*
2001 27 February: Silver Jubilee of St Mary's Primary School.
29 June: Canon Reid's Golden Jubilee.
2002 17 August: *140th anniversary of the opening of St Mary's Church, Patrick Street.*
Major renovations.
2008 *Bicentenary of the founding of the Greenock Mission.*

APPENDIX 2

PRIESTS OF ST MARY'S 1798-2002

NOTE: Missionary Rectors and Parish Priests are in **bold type**, and marked *
Dates of ordination are in *(italics)* followed by dates of service in St Mary's.

Abbé Simon Louis Capperon (Capron) c.1798-Died 27 Sept 1805.
Abbé Louis Lemonnier (Lemoine) c.1805-Died 1813.
Abbé Gilles-Vincent Despréaux 1813.

Rev.

* **John Davidson** *(1792)* ?Dec 1808. Died 8 Jan 1815.

* **John Gordon** (*1802*) 1816-resigned 1833. Died 26 Oct 1833.

John Gifford 1830. Went to Dumbarton.

Joseph Curr Jan-May 1832.

William Gordon (*1831*) May 1832-May 1836. Went to St Andrew's, Glasgow. Returned in 1852.

\+ **Bp Andrew Scott** (*1795*) 1834-Died 4 Dec 1846.

Alexander Smith (Later Bishop) (*1836*) 1836-Dec 1841. Went to Paisley. Died Glasgow 15 June 1861.

* **Peter Keenan** M.D. (*1838*) Aug 1840-Died 8 Aug 1843.

Michael Ryan (*1841*) 1841-1845. Later in Newton Stewart, then Glasgow. Recalled to Ireland. Died 1873.

John Kerr (*1835*) Oct 1843-Aug 1845. Died Dalbeth 2 Sept 1873.

John Gordon (*1841*) 1845-1846. Became mentally ill. Died in Ireland 1850.

* **James Danaher** (*1845*) 1845-April 1852. Went to St Andrew's, Glasgow, then Hamilton. Died 13 Nov 1886.

* **Richard Sinnott** M.D. b. Greenock (*1817*) Dec 1846-Died 19 Aug 1847.

Duncan McNab (*1845*) 1847-1848. Went to Australia. Died Melbourne 1896.

Joseph Manticha b. Greenock. (*1848*) April 1848-1849. Went to Eastern District. Died Portobello 31 Aug 1852.

William Casey (*1848*) Aug 1849-Aug 1850. Founded Girvan Mission. Went to America.

Francis Danaher (*1850*) May 1850-Feb 1852. Went to St Alphonsus', Glasgow, then Duntocher. Died Hamilton 5 Dec 1874.

Andrew Black (*1849*) Feb 1852-Aug 1854. Died Rothesay 21 April 1867.

* **William Gordon** (2) May 1852-Died 15 Dec 1880.

Charles F. Reid (*1846*) Aug 1854-June 1868. Went to Helensburgh. Died Rothesay 20 April 1886.

Hugh Chisholm Dec 1854-April 1855. (Later Provost, St Mirin's). Died Paisley 1908.

Hugh Gallagher (*1855*) Oct 1855-Feb 1856. Died 1897.

John J. Kyle D.D. Feb 1856-Jan 1858 (Later Canon, Preshome). Died 1873.

John Vassall Nov 1858-Oct 1859.

Michael Fox D.D. (*1863*) 1863-June 1867. Went to St Lawrence's. Died 1906.

* **Alexander Canon Taylor** (*1867*) 31 Aug 1867-Died 6 Jan 1905.

Donald Kennedy Oct 1868 (on loan from Northern District). Went to Drimnin, Morvern, June 1869. Died Fochabers 1925.

Hugh Macdonald June 1869-28 Aug 1870. Joined Redemptorists, later Provincial & Bp of Aberdeen. Died Edinburgh 1898.

William O'Shaughnessy Aug 1870-June 1872. Died Rutherglen 1897.

Patrick Byrne (*1872*) 1872-Jan 1873. Went to Largs. Recalled to Ireland. Died 1925.

"A magnificent specimen of Irish manhood, standing over 6 feet." (Dungarvan Observer).

Louis C. J. Macintyre (*1874*) 1874-June 1878. Went to Helensburgh, later Govan. Died Droitwich 1916.

Patrick Graham (*1878*) June 1878-March 1879. Returned to Ireland due to bad health.

Thomas J. Cunningham May 1879-Aug 1880. Went to Parkhead. Died Cambuslang 1891.

Humphrey O'Callaghan (*1880*) April 1880-14 Feb 1881. Went to Anderston.

Patrick Gaule (*1880*) 1880-1885. Went to Larkhall. Died Dublin 1932.

John Angland (*1880*) 1880-83. Later at Antwerp Cathedral. Died Glasgow 1920.

William P. O'Brien (*1883*) 31 Aug 1883-July 1888. Died 1937.

Louis C. DeBacker (*1881*) June 1885-Nov 1887. Went to Cadzow (Hamilton). Died Brussels 1932.

James F. Morrison (*1884*) 8 Nov 1888-April 1891. Died Torquay 1916.

Ellis P. Rogan D.D. (*1887*) July 1888-June 1890. Died Shieldmuir 1919.

Charles F. De Monti (*1889*) Sept 1890-May 1895. Died Klerksdorp, Transvaal, 1903.

Ludger W. Kuhler (*1889*) May 1891-17 Oct 1892. Returned to Germany.

David Morris (*1889*) 19 Nov 1892-29 June 1896. Went to Gourock.

James Carroll (*1890*) 19 Nov 1892-27 Oct 1896. Recalled to Ireland. Died 1941.

Alexr. McCormick July 1895-Aug 1895. Died Rothesay 1903.

Michael P. O'Connor Sept 1895-Oct 1895. Went to Dumbarton. Recalled to Ireland Died 1944.

Andrew Lynch (*1895*) 3 Oct 1895-June 1900. Died Glasgow 1936.

Charles E. Fleming (*1896*) 28 Sept 1896-Oct 1903. Went to Carluke. Died Ayr 1939.

Charles Mann (*1886*) 3 Nov 1896-Died 22 April 1901.

Stephen Thornton June 1900-Oct 1900. Died Glasgow 1936.
Thomas Gibbons (*1900*) 1901-1911. Recalled to Ireland. Died 1935.
Joseph O'Leary (*1901*) 1901-1905. Went to Motherwell.
Died Glasgow 1951.
James McDaid (*1903*) 1903-1908. Recalled to Ireland. Died 1943.
* **Patrick Canon Houlihan** (*1882*) Jan 1905-Died 4 Jan 1923.
Michael O'Donoghue (*1905*) 1905-1916. Recalled to Ireland. Died 1970.
William Browne (*1905*) 1905-1910. Recalled to Ireland. Died 1937.
William O'Connor (*1908*) July 1908-1912.
Died 1959 Dublin, buried Kilmarnock.
Michael Fitzpatrick (*1910*) 1910-1920. Recalled to Ireland. Died 1968.
Thomas Wall (*1911*) 1911-1919. Recalled to Ireland. Died 1935.
William Ryan (*1912*) 1912-1916. Volunteered as army chaplain.
Maurice O'Connor (*1915*) 1915-1921. Recalled to Ireland. Died 1952.
John Wall (*1916*) 1916-1925. Recalled to Ireland. Died 1928.
Cousin of Thomas above.
Peter J. McFarlane (*1908*) 1917-1919.
James Ronan (*1919*) 1919-1925. Recalled to Ireland.
John Scanlon (*1919*) 1919-1931. Later P.P., St Patrick's. Died 1964.
Daniel J. Horgan, jun. (*1919*) 1920-1924. Recalled to Ireland. Died 1958.
Michael Costello (*1920*) 1920-1925. Recalled to Ireland. Died 1967.
* **John Canon McMillan** (*1898*) 1923-Died 26 April 1945.
Aloysius McGurk (*1925*) 1925-1934. Went to Mossend.
Later retired to Ireland through ill-health. Died 11 January 1952.
Simon Hegarty (*1924*) 1925-1926. Went to Springburn,
later recalled to Ireland. Died Cork 1952.
William Christie 1925-1928.
James Phelan (*1924*) 1926-1927.
Daniel McGlinchy (*1927*) 1927-1929. Later Mgr, P.P. St Ninian's.
Died 28 August 1973.
Edward Dempsey (*1928*) 1928-1929. Died Glasgow 27 March 1962.
Gerald McDade (*1926*) 1929-1931 Died Dalmuir 22 July 1955.
John McLaughlin (*1929*) 1929-1944. Died Glasgow 3 Dec 1951.
William Mallon D.D. (*1929*) 1930-1933. Died Dalmuir 5 March 1973.
Michael McNicholas (*1927*) 1931-1933. Went to Parkhead.
Later P.P., St James', Paisley. Died 31 August 1959.
Francis Magauran, D.D. (*1925*) 1933-1943.
Later Monsignor. V.G. Paisley Diocese. Died 12 January 1975.
John O'Riordan (*1929*) 1934-1938. Went to Lambhill. Died 25 April 1975.
John Cusick (*1927*) 1936-1945. Died Law 7 Dec 1965.
Herbert G. Rogers (*1930*) 1938-1941.
Died Santa Monica, U.S.A. 25 August 1973.
John Ross (*1939*) 1939-1941.
Francis McLeod (*1937*) 1942-1944. Died Birkenhead 20 June 1977.
Thomas Brooks (*1927*) 1943-1946. Went to Bothwell. Died 2 May 1973.

Thomas McKeown (*1941*) 1943-1945. Died Glasgow 23 March 1981.
* **William Canon Horgan** (*1892*) 1945-1947. Retired to Ireland.
Died June 1948.
James Fisher (*1941*) 1945-1961. Later P.P. Linwood. Died 1979.
Daniel Horgan (*1927*) Nov-Dec 1946. Later P.P. St Lawrence's. Died 1979.
Nephew of Canon William above.
* **Henry E. Canon Hart** (*1923*) 1947-Died 26 Oct 1959.
Vincent Grace (*1934*) 1947-1950. Later P.P. Wemyss Bay.
Died 23 May 1978.
John Earley (*1940*) 1946-1951. Later P.P. St Aidan's, Johnstone.
Died 1 Jan 1987.
P. B. Molony (*1922*) 1950-1975. Retired to Ireland. Died 14 Feb 1978.
Matthew Dillon (*1949*) 1951-1958. Later Chaplain to Forces.
Recalled to Ireland.
* **John D. Canon Daniel** (*1923*) 1959-Died 28 Jan 1972.
Neil Duffin (*1958*) 1958-1967. Went to Lima, Peru. Later P.P., Elderslie.
Eamonn Drummond (*1960*) 1960. To St John's, P.G.
John McElroy (*1956*) 1961-1973 Later P.P. Eaglesham; Neilston.
James Cunningham (*1960*) 1964-1969. Later P.P. St James', Renfrew.
John Fitzsimmons (*1963*) 1966-1967. Later P.P. Erskine.
Joseph Logue (*1953*) 1969-1975. Later P.P. St Anthony's, Johnstone;
Bishopton.
Joseph Alexander (*1962*) 1975-1983. Later P.P. St Andrew's.
* **Mgr Hugh Gallagher** (*1945*) 1972-retired 1994.
James McGhee (*1962*) 1983-1989.
David Shankland (*1986*) 1989-1990.
Joseph Dow b. Greenock, (*1973, St Mungo's*) 1990-1994.
Went to St James', Renfrew.
Michael G. Sheridan (*1960*) 1987-1994.
Paul Cosh (*1990*) 1994-1996.
* **Andrew Carroll** (*1974*) Oct 1994-retired Sept 2000.
* **John Tormey** (*1981*) Sept 2000-

APPENDIX 3

From *The Directory to the Service of the Catholic Church. 1863*

OPENING OF ST MARY'S NEW CHURCH

The solemn opening of this magnificent Church, the aspect of which leads back in spirit to the glorious piles of the mediaeval ages, took place on Sunday the 17th August, within the Octave of the Assumption of our Blessed Lady, under whose powerful invocation this temple is dedicated to Almighty God. The blessing of the Church was performed privately in the morning by the Rev. W. Gordon P.P., who had received the necessary faculties for that purpose. Notwithstanding the high price of the tickets, the building was densely crowded in every part, when the procession, headed by cross-bearer and acolytes, emerged from the sacristy, and proceeded by the left aisle, and up the nave, to the High Altar.

Pontifical High Mass was then celebrated by the Right Rev. Dr Murdoch, the officiating clergy being - Assistant-Priest, the Very Rev. John Gray, V.G., and Coadjutor Bishop elect; Deacon, Rev. John McLachlan, of Kilmarnock; Sub-Deacon, Rev. James Boyle, of St Patrick's, Glasgow; Master of Ceremonies, Rev. Valentine Chisholm, of St John's, Glasgow. The Rev. W. Gordon, and Charles Reid, of St Mary's; the Rev. Michael Condon, of St Lawrence's, Greenock; the Rev. Alexander Munro, of Paisley.

After the Gospel, the Rev. Mr Munro delivered a most impressive discourse on "sacrificial worship," with special reference to the Catholic teaching and worship in the sacrifice of the Mass. To the very large number of Protestants who were present, this discourse must have proved most instructive and interesting. At the conclusion, the reverend preacher, looking upon the magnificent building in which they were assembled, as a munificent gift of the Catholics of Greenock to their children, called on them to complete the good work, by handing it down to their remotest posterity perfectly free and untrammelled from the incumrances of any sort, as a truly noble monument of their piety and generosity.

The music was Mozart's Mass, No.12, which was performed by the members of St Andrew's choir, Glasgow, who, under the able superintendence of the Rev. Alex. Reid, and aided by the Greenock choir, rendered the whole of this charming composition in a very creditable manner.

The church is built on the ancient plan consecrated by centuries of Christian usage, of a central nave with aisles, the former terminating in an apse which contains the sanctuary and the altar. Ranges of cylindrical columns with lofty bases, annulets, and sculptured capitals, support the arcades of pointed arches, which, wrought in parti-coloured stone, separate the nave from the aisles, and support the upper or clear story of the church. Both aisle and clear-story walls are pierced with windows of a simple, we may almost say, severe character, yet harmonising with the general effect of austere and masculine dignity which must strike every one who considers the building.

An arcade runs entirely round the clear-story wall, pierced with windows at intervals, and where blank, affording admirable space for paintings. The western end of the church is a fine composition of a wheel window and two long tracery windows, and below a double doorway of great breadth and solidity of character enclosed within a gabled projection, and enriched with a central niche upon a granite shaft and sculptured foliage.

The tower which flanks the gable of the nave is yet incomplete, and in its unfinished state is, we fear, a monument of the depressed state of trade in the country. With better times we hope to see it grow up and crown the edifice with its belfry.

Passing from the building proper to its furniture, we must remark first upon the elegant organ gallery, sustained on shafts of red Dumbarton stone, and with a delicately-pierced front, and most exquisite spiral staircase in wood-work, the latter being as elaborate and fine a piece of constructive carpentry as we ever saw. The nave and aisles are seated in commodious low open seats, which hardly obstruct the comprehensive view of the church.

A font of handsome design, and inscribed

"Qui crediderit et baptizatus fuerit salvus erit,"

stands below the tower. The altars and pulpits are evidently only temporary erections.

Eight stained-glass windows of great depth and richness of colour terminate the nave and aisles, representing the B. Virgin, St Patrick, St Andrew, and other saints beneath canopies, and surrounded by elaborate ornamental borders. The sanctuary, side chapels, and space about the font are laid with beautiful floors of encaustic tiles.

The Presbytery, or Clergy House, is approached from the church through the sacristy or vestiary, and the confessionals are connected with this apartment and the house by a short cloister. It is both spacious and commodious, without any greater indulgence than that of ample light and air, and contains a fine library, with the usual accommodations of a private gentleman's house. The staircase, with its elegant balustrade, panelled roof, and its arcade of lights, is a very striking feature.

The whole building, with its various details and ornamental fittings, was designed by and carried out under the directions of George Goldie Esq., of London, Architect. The plans have been skilfully and intelligently carried out by Mr Simpson, the contractor, Tottenham Court Road, London.

The stained glass is from the workshops of Mr Wailes, of Newcastle; the tiles from Messrs Maw's manufactory in Salop; Mr Earp, of London, has executed the sculpture; and Messrs Peard & Jackson, the elegant gas fittings.

The church measures 120 feet long by 60 feet wide, and 60 feet high, internal dimensions; it will seat 800 persons, exclusive of standing space and a large organ gallery, and the total cost of the whole building, including all the fittings, enclosure walls, stained glass, &c., &c., complete, is under £6000.

The former church has been converted into two large and excellent schools.

APPENDIX 4

A LIST OF ITEMS GIFTED TO ST MARY'S CHURCH, NOT MENTIONED IN THE BODY OF THE TEXT

Crib figures	:	Miss Maggie Bryceland
Lectern (1975)	:	In memory of Joe Stewart
Chairs for Sanctuary	:	James Orr
Cross	:	Legacy of Helen McGeehan
Chalice and ciborium	:	Robert & Rose McLachlan & Family
Chalice	:	In memory of Elizabeth McLachlan
Two chalices	:	In memory of Tony McElroy
Chalice	:	In memory of Celia Campbell
Chalice	:	In memory of Annie Gillespie
Chalice	:	In memory of Margaret Gallagher

This is as full a list as it was possible to draw up. Apologies for any omissions.

APPENDIX 5

Rev. John Davidson, the founder of the Greenock Mission, died on 8 January 1815. He was buried in the Sinnott family lair in the Old West Churchyard, along with one of his French predecessors, Rev. Louis Lemonnier, known locally as "Lemoine". When the Kirk was moved to the Esplanade the priests' remains were exhumed and reburied in Greenock Cemetery on 16 March 1927. (M. Capperon's burial place is not known.)

According to Rev. Michael Condon (the first priest of St Lawrence's) Lemoine's name was visible on the "fractured recumbent stone" until 1864 when the broken piece was removed, leaving only the words: "Dumusque 1792" *(until 1792).*

Condon surmises that this was "probably the last line of a Latin inscription, telling the pastorate or charge held in France by Father Lemoine until 1792, when the Revolution made him a refugee."[1]

A new stone was erected in 1927 to mark the the priests' final resting place in Greenock Cemetery. It is headed with the words "num usque 1792", apparently a misreading of the original.

Canon Condon closed his pamphlet on "The Catholic Church in Greenock" (1880) with a tribute to John Davidson:

THE UNREMEMBERED

Whilst autumn's tinted leaves were flying fast,
Into the old kirkyard I pensive passed;
And sought the spot where in its vesture lay,
With kindred dust, the consecrated clay.

Edged by a fragment, as "Dumusque" known —
Close by the kirk-wall was a nameless stone;
'Twas thine, poor Davidson's, by all forgot —
Alas! hast thou no friend? How strange thy lot!

It must not be. Again thy name shall rise
To gladden faithful hearts and brimful eyes —
Upon thy tomb, once more, thy flock shall trace
The "Requiescat" of a grateful race.

1. Rev. Michael Condon, *The Catholic Church in Greenock.*

BIBLIOGRAPHY

GREENOCK

Statistical Account of Scotland (1791-1799)

New Statistical Account of Scotland (1845)

Report on the State of the Irish Poor in Great Britain
(Royal Commission Investigation)1836

Minutes of Greenock Burgh School Board 1873

Brown Archibald, *Early Annals of Greenock*
(Orr, Pollock & Co., Greenock, 1905)

Donald John, *Old Greenock Characters*
(Milne, Tannahill & Methven, Perth: Series 1, 1920; Series 2, 1930)

Dow James L., *Greenock* (Greenock Corporation, 1975)

Hamilton T.W., *How Greenock Grew* (McKelvie & Sons Ltd, Greenock, 1947)

Mullen Diane, *The Irish in Greenock, 1841-187*
(Unpublished Dissertation, Glasgow Caledonian University, 2000.)

Snoddy T.G., *Round About Greenock*
(The Allen Lithograph Co. Ltd., Kirkaldy, 1950)

CATHOLIC CHURCH

The Catholic Directory for Scotland

Anson Peter F., *Underground Catholicism in Scotland*
(Standard Press, Montrose, 1970)

Canning Rev. Bernard J., *Irish-Born Secular Priests in Scotland*
(Bookmag, Inverness, 1979)

____, *The Diocese of Paisley, 1947-1997* (Diocese of Paisley, 2001)

Devine T.M., *St Mary's, Hamilton, a Social History 1846-1996*
(John Donald, Edinburgh, 1995)

Watts John, *Scalan, the Forbidden College* (Tuckwell Press, East Linton 1999)

The Memoirs of Canon Michael Condon
(Unpublished, Glasgow Archdiocesan Archives.)

Finance Board Minutes (Glasgow Archdiocesan Archives)

ARTICLES

Irish Geography (Magazine) 1971 Vol.6, No.3:
Lobban R.D., *The Irish Community in Greenock in the Nineteenth Century*

Innes Review:
Aspinwall Bernard, *The Formation of the Catholic Community in the West of Scotland* (1982 Pp.44-57)

____, *Children of the Dead End: the Formation of the Modern Archdiocese of Glasgow, 1815-1914* (1992 Pp.119-144)

____, *Scots and Irish Clergy Ministering to Immigrants, 1830-1878*
(Spring 1996 Pp.45-68)

ARTICLES (continued)
Johnson Christine, *Secular Clergy of the Lowland District, 1732-1829* (1983 Pp.79-86)
____, *Scottish Secular Clergy 1830-1878* (1989 Pp.106-152)
MacDonald Rev. Roderick, *Bishop Scott and the West Highlands* (Autumn 1966)
McGloin James, *Some Refugee French Clerics* (Spring 1965)
Walsh Rev. James, *Archbishop Manning's Visitation of the Western District of Scotland in 1867* (Spring 1967)
St Peter's College Magazine, Vol. 22, No. 87. December 1956:
Daniel V. Rev. John D., *St Laurence's* (sic), *Greenock*

BOOKLETS /PAMPHLETS
Anonymous, but certainly by Rev. Michael Condon:
The Catholic Church in Greenock, 1880
Anonymous, *Catholicity in Greenock, 1909* (Centenary Booklet)
Canning Rev. Bernard J., *Instruments of His Work* (Little Sisters Centenary Booklet, 1984)
Darragh James, *Bishop Andrew Scott* (C.T.S. Pamphlet, 1946)
McCurdy Joseph, *Roots* (Centenary of St Mary's School, East Shaw Street, 1978)
Murray Thomas P.F., *St Columba's High School Golden Jubilee*, 1983
A Cause for Rejoicing. (Franciscan Sisters Centenary Booklet, 1974)
Notre Dame High School. (Silver Jubilee Magazine, 1993)
St Mary's Youth Club Magazine, 1946
St Patrick's School, Greenock (Centenary Booklet, 1978)

NEWSPAPERS
Glasgow Observer
Catholic Herald
Greenock Advertiser
Greenock Telegraph
The Scottish Protestant

ST MARY'S ARCHIVES
Parish Registers
Sick Call Books
Notice Books
Minutes of Deanery Meetings
CYMS Minutes

UNPUBLISHED ARTICLES
Dalton Sister Eleanor, *SHM Sisters in Greenock*
Macdonald Michael, *Organ — St Mary's Church, Greenock*
McGeehan Martin, *St Mary's 2002 — The Steering Group — 1998 to 2001*
McLellan William B., *Society of St Vincent de Paul — St Mary's Conference, Greenock*